THE NEW
AMERICAN
KITCHEN
GARDEN

Shepherd Ogden

THE NEW
KITCHEN

AMERICAN GARDEN

**National Home
Gardening Club**
Minneapolis, Minnesota

The New American Kitchen Garden

Vice President, Product Marketing/Business Development
Mike Vail

Vice President, Continuity and Merchandise Marketing
Cal Franklin

Book Products Development Manager
Steve Perlstein

Home Gardener's Library Executive Editor
A. Cort Sinnes

Developmental Editor
Ken Burke

Content Editor
Paul Peterson

Copy Editor
Ellen Hatfield

Photo Editor
Jennifer Block

Series Design, Art Direction and Production
David J. Farr, ImageSmythe

Photo Credits

William D. Adams: 46, 66, 69, 71, 74, 75, 82, 96 (2), 100, 101, 102, 104 (3), 111, 115, 122; Gary Braasch: 48; David Cavagnaro: 57, 65, 68, 70, 78, 82, 83 (2), 84, 85 (3), 86 (2), 88, 90, 92, 95 (3), 97, 98, 105, 111, 113 (2), 115 (3), 116 (2), 121 (2); Walter Chandoha: 9, 20 (2), 58, 60, 61, 63, 64, 65, 71, 72, 73, 74, 76 (2), 77, 79, 81, 82, 86 (2), 89, 90 (4), 92, 93, 94, 99 (2), 100, 102 (2), 103, 105, 110, 112 (2), 113, 114, 115, 116 (2), 118, 121, 123; Rosalind Creasy: 12, 18 (2) 19, 21 (2), 41, 44, 49, 52, 53 (3), 56 (2), 57, 59, 62, 69, 70, 74, 75, 77, 78, 84 (2), 87 (2), 90 (2), 93 (2), 96, 97, 105, 106, 107 (2), 110, 117; Thomas E. Eltzroth: 64, 65, 75, 83, 86, 87, 93, 97, 100, 108; Derek Fell: Cover, 2, 3, 4, 7, 16, 17, 22, 23 (2), 26, 39, 41, 42, 50, 62, 63, 66, 75, 78, 80, 81, 86, 90, 96, 98, 100, 102, 104, 106, 107, 109, 110, 114 (2), 120 (2), 122; Saxon Holt: 10, 18, 36, 38, 43, 49, 51, 77, 92, 102, 104; Jeff Johnson: 124, 125, 126, 127 (2), 128, 129, 130, 131 (2), 132, 133, 134 (2), 135, 136; Michael Landis: 6, 11, 15; Hugh Palmer: viii, 5, 8, 13, 14, 21, 22, 23, 62, 85, 87 (2), 89, 90, 91, 93; Jerry Pavia: 21, 23, 40, 42, 47, 73, 80, 87, 88 (2), 95, 112 (2); Robert Perron: 13; Stephen R. Swinburne: 1, 10, 54, 84; Mark Turner: 78, 84, 87, 94, 105, 117, 120 (2).

ISBN 0-914697-75-7

National Home Gardening Club
12301 Whitewater Drive
Minnetonka, Minnesota 55343

CONTENTS

CHAPTER 4

KITCHEN GARDEN PLANT GUIDE 61

CHAPTER 5

SEASONAL RECIPES FOR THE KITCHEN GARDEN 125

THE NEW
AMERICAN
KITCHEN
GARDEN

WHAT MAKES A KITCHEN GARDEN?
WHAT MAKES IT *YOURS?*

"I'm putting in our new kitchen garden this year."
"Terrific idea!...Er, what's a kitchen garden?"

Perhaps without realizing it, people have enjoyed some form of "kitchen gardening" for thousands of years. In fact, there have been so many types of kitchen gardens in so many civilizations that boundaries blur. Each generation adapts the cumulative eating and healing habits, and the garden and plant lore, of its ancestors. Add countless ethnic, cultural, culinary, and climatic adaptations and variations, and you might despair of ever coming up with a usable definition of "kitchen garden".

Fear not—we have a definition. To us, a kitchen garden reflects what gardeners all across North America have discovered, just recently or centuries ago. It's this: If you want the freshest food, the best food, and the handiest food, you'd better grow it yourself, and grow it right. Today we want to live healthier, be good to the earth, and enjoy the wonderful mix of tastes, flavors and scents that defines us as American gardeners. Creating a kitchen garden lets us do all of those things.

It's not as hard as it may sound. With a little planning, some pretty enjoyable work, and nature as your partner, you can have a fantastic, fun and fulfilling kitchen garden.

Today in America, we want to create gardens that fit our needs, resources, and style of living. We'll give you a little help in these pages so you can do just that. To create your own special kitchen garden, just follow a few basic guidelines.

❶ Your kitchen garden should be close to your house, preferably right next to your kitchen door, your patio or your outdoor eating area. It will be handiest there; besides, it will look wonderful. Keep it in view of the living areas in which you spend the most time.

❷ It should be a dedicated space, just for the things you like to eat, see, smell, or touch. That could mean several good-sized containers for your favorite patio plants, or it can mean a bigger enclosed family plot, or something in between. Because it contains your favorite plants, you should protect it from the elements and the critters.

❸ It should be productive, to allow you to grow a lot in a confined space. It should help you grow a variety of plants—vegetables, herbs, fruits, and flowers—both for eating and for enjoyment in and of themselves. Your kitchen garden should have well-drained, fertile soil that provides the nutrition to grow healthy plants rapidly. Your soil must hold its fertility through successive plantings and rotations.

❹ It should be of a manageable size. It should be low maintenance, so you can enjoy its bounty, instead of tending to endless needs and chores. It should make its harvest handy, with ample paths and ergonomically-sized beds that contain tendable plants and quickly-plucked produce.

❺ Finally, it should be both practical and aesthetically pleasing. After all, you're going to spend a lot of time in and near it. It should express your overall living design and be integral to your gardening, entertaining, and living preferences.

GARDEN DAYDREAMS

Can you conjure an image of yourself surrounded by a white picket fence, with compost-rich raised beds full of luscious carrots, scallions, and salad greens, or herbs and flowers to use in cooking or in making gifts? Do you love the gratification of popping out the kitchen door to snip fresh Italian parsley and sweet, pungent basil, to pluck succulent tomatoes and cool cucumbers, and pick nasturtium leaves and lavender flowers to make your salad perfect? Would you like to toss that salad with your own raspberry and opal basil vinaigrette, or give bottles of it to your friends at celebration time? Would you like to pick tender asparagus right from the border of your garden or smackingly sweet red raspberries from your garden's hedge?

Can you imagine special containers full of vegetables and flowers on your patio or porch, accenting and defining your eating, relaxing, and entertaining areas? If the rat race makes you seek respite, how about a private walled enclosure in the style of a monastery herbal and kitchen garden, where you can find "peas and quiet"?

Think of the homey, generous cuisine of the South: Chewy, steaming herbal cornbread, a big mess o' greens, filé gumbo, dirty rice, pulled pork sandwiches, fresh mint juleps. Maybe you see yourself creating a Southwest salsa garden within ageless adobe walls with a dozen kinds of volcanic chili peppers, heirloom tomatoes, onions, garlic, oregano, and Anasazi and pinquito beans. Or, how about a "kiss the chef" specialty garden right next to your barbecue, with plenty of onions, garlic, spuds, eggplant, tomatoes, and peppers ready for you to pop on the grill with your steak, salmon, hot dogs or tofu!

Shepherd Ogden

Imagine yourself sitting on your porch swing on a balmy evening with your special loved one, eating blueberry pie with berry-stained fingers and smelling the heady scents of moonflowers and flowering tobacco from your nearby garden borders.

If any of these mental pictures makes you feel good, then you deserve the rewards of a kitchen garden. And this book will help you create a new American kitchen garden that's your very own.

—SHEPHERD OGDEN

Chapter 1

CREATING A NEW ERA IN KITCHEN GARDENING

The modern American kitchen garden is coming back into its own as part of a long tradition of people seeking a measure of self-sufficiency and individual style. In terms of importance and good looks, today's kitchen garden can hold its own with any lush flower border or velvety front lawn. It distinguishes itself from the rambling "back-40" grow-everything vegetable patch because ❶ it concentrates on flavorful, high-yield, intensively-grown plants, and ❷ it is an attractive and integral part of your overall garden and outdoor living space, as opposed to being planted in some remote or hidden corner of the yard. It's a garden to be proud of!

One great thing about kitchen gardens is that space doesn't matter. You can grow your kitchen garden in a postage-

Much too attractive to hide away, in some far corner of your backyard, plan your kitchen garden close to your back door.

One of the basic principles of kitchen gardening is to get maximum use out of whatever space you have available. This often means closer than normal planting and rotating crops.

stamp sized bed…in a group of containers on a patio…in a decent-sized bed right next to your porch or picnic table…or in a large family plot intent on big-time production.

Many think of the kitchen garden as a family garden, because it provides a focus for family activity and a center of gravity for the perennial activities of food, work, mutual assistance and learning—activities that hold a family together so pleasurably. But gardening, especially kitchen gardening, is just as fulfilling to couples, groups of friends, and single people. For many of us today, our "family" may not be relatives per se, but friends and loved ones all the same. We share our lives with them. We wish to please them, so we entertain them, we cook for them and with them, and we break bread with them. We show love through giving. Kitchen gardens help us give—in a very direct, personal way.

Trellises add an interesting visual angle to a kitchen garden, and actually add space for planting while enhancing eye-appeal at the same time. ❧

THE ORIGINS OF THE KITCHEN GARDEN

The garden of the type we discuss in this book has truly ancient origins. Depictions of gardens with many of the same characteristics as today's show up in Egyptian paintings dated circa 3000 B.C. The Persians created the garden as an oasis and developed the concept of enclosed enjoyment. (The word "paradise" is a Persian word for garden.) The Romans had extensive villa gardens that provided both food for the kitchen, and a pleasure ground for relaxation and entertainment of visitors. As the Romans conquered new lands, all across Europe and into the British Isles, they brought their ideas of kitchen gardening with them.

The oldest existing plans for a type of kitchen garden are from a Swiss monastery garden and are dated A.D. 820! The 16th-century gardens in Padua, Italy are considered the model for many later examples of the art in Europe, and then America. English writers like

Above One of the best things about raised beds is that they can be filled with whatever soil type the crop requires.
Opposite Any kitchen garden relies on well-defined beds and borders which helps keep maintenance to a minimum.

Kitchen gardens have a long history in Europe as witnessed by this late 19th century walled garden in England.

Thomas Hill, author in 1563 of *The Proffitable Arte of Gardening*, were firm adherents of ancient designs and methods wherein relatively large, modular plots of vegetables were surrounded by narrow borders of flowers and herbs inside an outer fence or wall to form an aesthetic, and usually geometric, whole.

As the Renaissance gave way to the Enlightenment, however, kitchen gardens became more systematized and segregated. They were relegated to a separate part of the garden, ultimately leading to the very pragmatic gardens of the mid-20th century that stressed only practical considerations at the cost of losing aesthetic ones.

KITCHEN GARDENS AND VICTORY GARDENS

After World War II, vegetable gardens declined in America, shrinking in size and importance as we became consumers of mass-produced food along with other mass-produced goods. During both of the world wars, there were victory gardens. A lot of food was produced by home gardeners, more out of a sense of duty and obligation than from the love of fresh food or from the simple joy of gardening.

With the postwar rise of the year-round, nationally based food system—with production, primarily in the south and west, shipped to the rest of the nation—there seemed no reason to keep growing vegetables, not even to save money, because it became cheaper (in cash terms) to buy food, rather than grow it.

But in just the last 20 years or so, vegetable gardening (*all* gardening, in fact) has been on the upswing. Some experts say it is the aging of the baby boomers and a new interest in life at home. We have greener, less frenetic pursuits in general—more walks

Right Every inch of space should be used in a kitchen garden including border plantings on both sides of an enclosing fence. Above Here a mild climate favors a planting of citrus. Opposite If you are concerned about minimizing the maintenance your kitchen garden requires, by all means install raised beds.

together in the park or the woods. More board games, reading, or playing music, more gardening and cooking—even in households without children.

Whatever it is, we seem to benefit from the contact of hand to land—the warm sun on our backs as we weed, the lilting song of a bird perched on an overhead tree, the memory of planting the seed as we pick the peas. The awareness of wind and weather as we work late in

Even a small kitchen garden will yield a surprisingly large harvest.

the afternoon, watching the swallows swoop low to catch the insects weighted down by incipient rain, helps us know, in our bones, that today is the day to harvest. We look ahead, knowing that tomorrow will be a day to stay out of the garden as the rain falls, so we don't spread the freshly germinated spores of the fungi on the leaves of the plants.

As a firsthand way of experiencing nature, gardens have become a respite from the hustle and bustle of our busy, over-committed lives. A garden is a place where we can regain a *quality* of life that recently seemed lost to the modern

*Left The restored kitchen gardens surrounding the 16th century Chateau de Villandry are amongst the most extravagant in all of Europe. **Below** With a little extra effort even rooftop gardeners can have a kitchen garden.*

Above A small space is no impediment to creating a wonderful collection of your favorite edibles. Left Kitchen gardens have a long history in America, witnessed by George Washington's restored garden at Mount Vernon.

quantity of life. Gardening adds quality to our lives on a daily basis. The cumulative sum of this daily quality brings us great personal satisfaction.

RECAPTURING QUALITY IN OUR FOOD

There also has been a new interest in both healthy food and clean food, which leads directly to the vegetable garden and then to the kitchen. Media reports are full of distressing accounts of contaminated, unhealthy or simply un-nutritious foods. By taking charge of as much of our food as we can—from beginning to end, seed to table—we can be sure that we are doing all we can to provide ourselves and our loved ones the best

food possible. Quickly, we see the remarkable difference between food we grow ourselves, harvest at the peak of perfection, and cook with craft and care, and the mass-produced, bred-to-be-shipped, shelf-life-stabilized, irradiated produce in the supermarket.

This grounding—this connection—is the reason we are drawn to gardening, especially kitchen gardening.

In this book we will help you create a personal connection by examining the amazing variety of today's kitchen gardens and by helping you custom-design a garden to fit your own needs, resources, and preferences, no matter how much time or how much space you have.

Chapter 2

PLANNING AND DESIGNING THE KITCHEN GARDEN

The first question you have to ask yourself when considering what kind of kitchen garden you want is, "What kind of cook am I?" It is the close connection between the kitchen and the garden that defines its purpose, and what is grown there. What you like to cook will even, to a degree, determine the design of your kitchen garden.

Ask yourself these kinds of questions. Do you like salads—lots of tender juicy vegetables plucked in their youth. . . crunchy radishes. . .tiny, crisp, sweet carrots. . .fresh scallions. . .flavorful herbs. . . and the luscious sunny warmth of vine-ripe melons and tomatoes—a garden of seasonal delight? Or are you partial to putting up crops for the winter—larger carrots. . .onions, garlic and shallots . . .plump, hardy beets. . .earthy potatoes

If predators, such as dogs and deer, aren't a problem, the height of the enclosure of your kitchen garden isn't important.

. . . even celery root and parsnips, perhaps? Do you like dried beans and all the gnarly and grotesque, but flavorful, winter squashes that make such hearty soups on brisk afternoons?

So many of us are refining our eating habits. Are you intent on eating a healthier diet and dumping junk foods? Are you evolving towards being vegetarian? Or are you cutting down on fats and seeking more healthy pursuits? Perhaps you're trying to lose some weight. Then your kitchen garden helps you doubly—with both healthy food and moderate exercise!

Some other questions: What are your own taste preferences and those of your family? There is no point in growing four bushels of parsnips if no one will eat them.

For example, do you especially love Italian cooking, or Mexican food? How about the zesty flavors of Thailand . . . the cuisine of Provence . . . down-home American cookin'?

Do you want to make fresh Eggplant Parmesan . . . chilis Rellenos . . . spicy stir-fry vegetables or curries . . . mixed salad greens with edible flowers, tossed with your own raspberry vinaigrette . . . charcoal-grilled veggie kabobs? Each of these implies different crops, different rotations and different allocations of space.

As a part of your inventory, don't forget to take into account the kinds of herbs and seasonings you use, and what flowers you want, whether for the table or for dried decoration and gifts at festive times.

Also of critical importance: how many are you? Single, or a retired couple with an empty nest? You might want a smaller garden. On the other hand, you might have lots more time and dedication to tend a larger plot, and a desire to share produce with neighbors or charitable causes. Or is yours a growing family with big needs, but also plenty of strong backs? The old kitchen gardens of the European gentry might have had many mouths to feed, but they also had many hands to help out when there was extra work to be done in spring or during harvest time.

How do you entertain and relax? Do your friends come over to unwind after work on Fridays? Do your children or grandchildren arrive hungry on Sunday afternoon? Do your buddies come over to play cards or croquet, badminton or bocce? These times call for food and entertaining. The size of your circle will affect the size of your garden!

A GARDENING INVENTORY

Your most important gardening tools at this stage are a pencil and pad of

Top and Opposite One of the best things about having a kitchen garden is having ready access to produce not available in your local markets, like this mesclun salad and heirloom tomato tart. *Above* The pleasures of a kitchen garden can live on long after the harvest.

Tending a kitchen garden puts you in touch with the many moods of summer.

and the desert, winter may be the best time for crops.

When do you have the time and interest to garden? Are you a schoolteacher with a large period of time available in the summer, or do you run a marina at a popular summer lake resort and work dawn to dusk from May to October? Do you work days or nights? Indoors or out? When—both in terms of the weeks and months, but also the days and nights—will you be most in the garden?

The climate also affects design of the kitchen garden in other ways. Every garden is affected by both macro- and microclimates. Fences, walls, shade, humidity, wind direction and intensity—all create a local microclimate that experienced gardeners will come to recognize and use to their advantage.

For example, do you have a sunny spot against a wall, a fence or side of the house, a place where you've set a bench or chair because you know it's located out of the cold winds and catches the sun, even in late winter? Well, you have identified a favorable microclimate. Your tender plants will enjoy that spot too! With practice, you may learn that you can place tender plants there two weeks earlier than on the north side of the same barrier!

STYLE AND MATERIALS

Besides climate and your available time, other factors affect both the look and the location of your kitchen garden. What style is your house? You may want to

For many good cooks, the most important crops in a kitchen garden are the culinary herbs.

paper. Make an inventory of your gardening needs and preferences: vegetables, fruits or berries, herbs, and flowers. Write down or chart out what you want.

The next step is to assess what you have. Look around at the space you have for gardening. Is there a sunny flower bed next to the porch that would be a perfect location for a kitchen garden? Do you have a mundane suburban backyard that begs for more fruitful use than an expanse of high-maintenance lawn? Do the plans for your new patio or deck give you room for plenty of good large containers for kitchen plants?

Once you've put together your needs and wants, it's time to examine your space, time and budget options and define your kitchen garden. That way your garden will fit your yard as well as the needs of your kitchen.

CLIMATE AND SEASON

Also important is the seasonality of your garden, which is itself related to your climate. When are growing conditions the best? We tend to think of gardens as summer places, but in the Deep South

Although some gardeners prefer a combination of both lawn and and other garden spaces, this enterprising cook decided she preferred edibles and flowers to a grassy front yard.

Nasturtiums offer both a hint of color in the yard, and edible flowers.

Tender salad greens and spring blossoms signal the beginning of the kitchen garden harvest.

Any low evergreen hedge provides a formal look for dividing beds.

make the garden consistent with the rest of your property—or not. Your kitchen garden may be where you depart from style. Whatever you decide, remember that as a visible and integral part of your yard, the style of your kitchen garden will have an effect on the rest of your outdoor living area.

Of further concern are the types of construction materials available in your area. In the arid West, adobe is a common material; in most parts, bricks and stone and bark (for paths) are abundant. Local availability of building materials and price will have an effect on the design of your garden.

DESIGN

The basic principles of kitchen garden design have been around for a very long time. They come down to a few simple rules of thumb that, when combined with the results of the kitchen gardening self-survey above, will result in a specific plan, ideally suited to your own situation and needs.

ENCLOSING YOUR GARDEN

Traditionally, kitchen gardens have been enclosed, both to protect the crops from

Deterring Destructive Deer

*D*EER CAN BE A BIG GARDENING PROBLEM, and not just in the countryside. They can quickly and thoroughly destroy a garden in the suburbs and even the city. If you have deer feeding in your area, the most effective preventive measure is a fence around your luscious kitchen garden to keep them out.

Any deer fence must be built tightly to the ground, because deer would rather crawl under a fence than jump over it. Fawns can get through a six-inch gap! The fence should be tall enough to prevent a mature deer from jumping over it—that's eight feet high at a minimum.

Where building an eight-foot-high enclosure isn't practical, you can construct a fence four or five feet tall, and closely plant evergreens inside it. Because deer won't jump into a spot they can't see, this creates a visual barrier. You can vary this method by building two parallel four- to five-foot fences, and plant a row of evergreens between them. This method is effective because it discourages deer from leaping over such a broad expanse.

If kids and pets are not around, consider using electric deer fencing, which needs only four feet of height to work. It's constructed with three parallel lines of 14-gauge wire—one line at 18 inches, one at 30 to 36 inches, and one along the top. Deer generally don't try to jump over electric fences, but stick their heads in and get a mild, startling shock and avoid the area.

---

pests and pilferage, and to temper the effects of climate. Whether this enclosure is in the form of a wall, a fence, a hedge—or even some sort of planting like blueberries, raspberries, or asparagus—the point is to define the garden as separate from the surrounding world. In the old days, the garden was separate from the wilderness, but today, it's just as likely that it is the city you want to keep out!

Walls

Each type of enclosure material is different. Walls made of stone or brick or adobe are favored for the ability to store large amounts of thermal energy. They hold heat gained from the sun both spring and fall, thus extending the normal growing season of crops planted near them (especially those facing south and west). Old-time gardeners have known for generations that such walls are used to provide a place to grow out-of-season fruits trained up the south or west face of the wall.

Walls do have two potential drawbacks, though: of all the barriers they are the most expensive; additionally, a solid wall, while it blocks the wind extremely

effectively, tends to create turbulence (in most cases, around 30 inches from the wall). This can be of real harm to susceptible plants within this narrow zone and needs to be taken into consideration at planting time.

Fences

Fences are more economical than walls, and can be designed to overcome the problem of wind turbulence. A partly porous fence, such as a picket fence or lattice, allows just enough air through to still air currents while blocking the major force of the wind. Unfortunately, fences do not provide the heat benefits of solid walls. One possible solution (which we use in our own garden) is to have some porous and some solid fence, and to use the south side of the solid portions for trellising tender plants.

Hedges

As beautiful as they are, hedges may not be the most practical solution for enclosing your kitchen garden. Whether they consist of strictly ornamental plants, or herbs, fruits or vegetables, they have

Expensive, but to many people worth it, a tall wall constructed of weathered brick provides the classic sense of enclosure for kitchen gardens.

Fences such as this wood and brick combination not only protect the garden, but make a design statement.

A split-rail fence does little to protect the garden from predators, but it adds a touch of rustic charm.

their own strengths and weaknesses. An evergreen hedge cuts cold winter winds without creating turbulence, but takes up considerably more room than a fence or a wall for a given height. Also, the hedge itself will be taking nutrients from any plants that are nearby.

Smaller, deciduous hedges will not be as effective in cutting the wind, and none of the hedges, unless specifically planted and maintained to do so, will keep out roving animals—one of the biggest garden pests.

Edible hedges—primarily herbs or flowers, normally less than 18 inches high—are best used as interior dividers to separate one part of the garden from another. Along with trellises and other vertical structures, they can provide the visual structure of the garden. A low fruiting hedge may be a good choice if you want fruit and have no better location for it.

Stakes not only provide critical support for plants, but they add vertical interest to the garden as well.

Although relatively high maintenance, hedges are among the most garden-friendly ways to divide up a garden.

CREATING FORM FOR THE GARDEN

An important principle in the creation of a kitchen garden is that it have at least a semi-permanent form—created from the shape of the beds, the edgings, and the pathways between them. The classic kitchen gardens of Europe had permanent paths and beds, quite often with four or more large plots that would be planted to vegetables, and then a number of smaller, often encircling, beds for flowers, herbs, or fruit.

For example, instead of just taking a large, rototilled space and planting it to long, mechanical-looking rows, why not create a set of planting areas (squares, rectangles, or curvilinear spaces) defined by paths and borders? Then, work within those defined planting beds. Not only will the garden be more beautiful, but rotating crops from bed to bed—a good gardening practice—will be easier to accomplish.

FINDING THE RIGHT LOCATION

Your kitchen garden needs to be located as close to the kitchen as possible. By doing so, you'll find that you'll use it and enjoy it constantly! On small lots that existed in colonial American villages, and still exist today in many towns, this is not much of a problem. By all means, resist the tendency to put the kitchen garden out behind the garage, or out on the "back 40". For the greatest enjoyment and use, integrate your kitchen garden into the landscape immediately surrounding your house. Believe me, you'll be glad you did.

SELECTING YOUR GARDEN PLANTS

Making a specific plan for what you'll actually plant is essential for any garden, and is particularly important here. The kitchen garden's space is more limited and its purpose is more defined. The smaller your space, the more important having a good sense of how you'll use space becomes.

Start your planting list by filling in the following checklist with basic information about your climate and your needs.

1. the space you have available for crops
2. how much you hope to harvest
3. first planting date
4. last hard freeze
5. last frost date
6. peak heat
7. first frost
8. hard freeze date

For many gardeners, the fun of a kitchen garden begins long before the first seeds are planted, since catalogues offer new varieties every year.

Yields of Fruits and Vegetables (25 ft. rows)		
Crop	**Yield**	**Notes**
Asparagus	8–10 lbs	Over six week harvest
Beans, Dry	25 lbs.	
Beans, Green	25 lbs.	For freezing and canning.
Beans, Green	10 lbs.	Baby "filet" beans
Beets	25–35 lbs.	
Broccoli	25 lbs.	
Brussels Sprouts	5 lbs.	
Cabbage	40–50 lbs.	
Carrots	25 lbs.	For mature harvest.
Carrots	15–20 lbs.	Baby carrots
Cauliflower	20–25 lbs.	
Celeriac	10–15 lbs.	
Celery	20–25 bchs.	
Cress	3–5 lbs.	
Cucumbers	25–35 lbs.	
Dandelion	3–5 lbs.	
Eggplant	20–25 lbs.	Less in cool climates
Endive	20–25 lbs.	
Garlic	40–50 bulbs	
Kale	25–40 lbs.	Multiple harvests
Kohlrabi	15–20 lbs.	
Leeks	20–25 lbs.	
Lettuce	15–20 lbs.	Left to mature
Lettuce	3–5 lbs.	Cut for mesclun
Mache	3–5 lbs.	
Mustard	25–40 lbs.	Left to mature
Mustard	3–5 lbs.	Cut for mesclun
Onions	25–40 lbs.	
Parsnips	25–30 lbs.	
Peas	8–10 lbs.	
Peppers	10–20 lbs.	Less in cool climates
Potatoes	25 lbs.	
Pumpkins	50–75 lbs	Depending on type
Radishes	8–10 lbs.	
Shallots	15–20 lbs.	
Spinach	10–20 lbs.	Depending on size at harvest
Squash, summer	5–25 lbs.	Depending on size at harvest
Squash, winter	35–40 lbs.	
Sweet Corn	25–30 ears	Plant at least four rows
Tomatoes	25–30 lbs.	
Turnips	15–25 lbs.	Depending on type

These yields assume high fertility and plant density.

If you don't have such climatic information handy, call your county extension agent. Most offices have horticulturists on hand to answer your questions.

For example, in a good year here in Vermont, we get about a pound of potatoes per square foot. Our family of four eats 200 to 300 pounds a year, so we know we need to dedicate a four- to six-foot by 50-foot bed to meet our potato harvest. Other examples: We've learned over the years that we eat about five to 10 linear feet of salad greens a week for as long as they are available. A three-foot-wide bed of spinach, 25 feet long, planted with three rows, will provide us with the frozen spinach we need for the winter months. Thus, after only a small amount of soul (and belly) searching, we can see if what we want matches what is possible. If not, we see that we have to adjust our planting plans, our expectations, or the size of our garden.

PLANNING AHEAD

Of course, not all crops occupy their space for the whole season, so you can squeeze in a little extra if you take the time to figure out crop successions and companion plantings. A number of these will be discussed in the next chapter, but just to give you the idea: We plant our peas in a closely spaced pair of rows, down the center of a three-foot raised bed with one row of spinach along each edge. By the time the peas have grown large enough to need the full bed, the spinach has been harvested. When the peas are done in mid-summer, we replace them with broccoli for fall harvest—right in the same bed.

We try to do all this figuring within the overall rotation plan for the garden, which dictates that crops in the same family, or that make similar demands on the soil, should not be grown in the same plot two years in a row. You can get very elaborate with rotation plans, but we keep it simple. Here's a rule of thumb to rotate a bed in succession: In a given bed, first plant leaf crops, then fruit crops, then root crops, and then legumes.

RECAPPING THE GARDEN BASICS

Briefly, a kitchen garden should be:

❶ As close to the kitchen as possible.
❷ Made from materials that best suit your needs and your budget (the least expensive materials are those that are locally available).

It's amazing how much production you can get from a relatively small space, especially if you use raised beds filled with top-quality soil and use a close planting scheme.

Once I had a gardener call me from New York City, asking how to pollinate corn. I explained the process, but intrigued, asked why he wanted to know.

"I have a penthouse in the city, and all my adult life I have wanted to have fresh sweet corn like I've read about."

"But where will you grow it?" I asked.

"I've got five plants in a half wine barrel, and I want to make sure the ears fill out, so I'm planning to hand pollinate them, then tell my wife to invite our two best friends over for dinner next month."

But is this kitchen gardening? You bet—of the most determined kind!

---

❸ Large enough to supply the gardener's family (however that may be defined), and yet small enough to manage realistically, so that it doesn't become a burdensome chore.

❹ In harmony with both your climate and the style of your property—unless you wish to depart from or expand your style.

Most of all, it should reflect your food needs and preferences.

HOW LARGE IS LARGE ENOUGH?

How large should your kitchen garden be? Go back to your inventory of needs, wants, and preferences, review your available space, and consult the plant encyclopedia in the next chapter to determine the space each plant takes. You may have more space than you expected, or you may need to compromise on your wish list, or cut across the board.

Remember that it isn't necessary to create the entire garden at once. In fact, it might make more sense to come up with an overall plan for the space you have available, and then develop the plan in a series of two or three phases over a few years. Nobody ever said that you have to plant everything you want the first year you try!

SAMPLE KITCHEN GARDEN PLANS

As gardeners, we want to create our own little bit of heaven on earth (or in the earth). As such, it may be useful to look at a few sample plans you can use as models.

A Large Family Garden (about 7200 sq. ft.)

As an example, let's start with a large family garden, like my own in southern Vermont. We are a family of four, who want to grow as much of our own vegetables, herbs, small fruits and flowers (for the table) as possible, both for fresh harvest and for storage.

We live on a relatively steep, south-facing hillside. Just below the house, along the driveway, is a saddle about 60 by 120 feet, sloping gently to the southwest, except in the lowest corner, where it drops away fairly quickly. Above and behind the house, the land is forested and steep.

Because of its good access to the house, we built our garden on the saddle. At the lower corner, we built a low retaining wall, then filled behind it to give it a consistent gentle slope over the whole plot. We adopted a double four-square plan, split by a wide path leading from the driveway to the tool shed—just large enough to accommodate our pickup truck.

At one end, we put modular, timber-edged plots of 12 by 20 feet for vegetables, and (as a vertical accent and for the fruit) semi-dwarf apple trees in the center of each plot.

At the other end are two more beds of the same size, one for my wife Ellen's medicinal herb garden, and one bed for the children's garden. In the children's plot, we built a small playhouse with a lookout tower, being careful to situate it so that its shade is beneficial to our plants' needs (lettuce, greens, spinach, etc.). Flanking the approach to the tool shed, we sited a variety of other modu-

Crops Sorted by Maturity Rate					
One Monthers **(<60 days)**	**Two Monthers** **(60-90 days)**		**Three Monthers** **(>90 days)**		
Spinach	Lettuce	Corn	Pole Beans	Garlic	Parsnips
Radishes	Beets	Scallions	Tomatoes	Shallots	Br. Sprouts
Salad Greens	Carrots	Potatoes	Peppers	Squashes	Beets
(Mesclun)	Endive	Broccoli	Eggplants	Melons	Carrots
Lettuce	Peas	Cabbage	Corn	Pumpkins	Potatoes
Kohlrabi	Bush Beans	Cauliflower	Onions	Parsley	

This is just a sample listing, based on our garden and using transplants wherever appropriate.

Plants Grouped By Plant Family *(and thus subject to similar problems)*						
Squash Family	**Mustard Family**	**Tomato Family**	**Beet Family**	**Legumes**	**Onion Family**	**Carrot Family**
Melons	Broccoli	Tomatoes	Beets	Beans	Onions	Carrot
Squash	Br. Sprouts	Eggplants	Spinach	Peas	Leeks	Dill
Cucumber	Cabbage	Peppers	Chard		Scallions	Parsnips
Pumpkins	Cauliflower	Potatoes			Garlic	Parsley
	Kohlrabi				Shallots	
	Kale					
	Mustard					
	Radishes					
	Turnips					

lar and symmetrical-shaped beds for asparagus, lilies, strawberries, and such.

We fenced the uphill and northwest sides with solid stockade fencing (to keep out deer and other varmints), backed with shrubs, and enclosed the downhill and southwest sides with a four-foot picket fence ringed with herbaceous perennial flower beds. This arrangement blocks chilly winds in spring, fall and winter. The porous picket fence not only helps frosty air to escape, but admits the cooling summer breezes that spring up in August.

Inside of the fences on the uphill side of the garden is a four-foot-wide perimeter bed for flowers and perennial food plants. There is also a flower border outside the picket fence that is dappled with fragrant plants, whose scent is picked up by the slightest breeze and distributed across the garden (and into the house).

To construct the beds we used four-inch by eight-inch timbers from a local sawmill. To help raise the soil level inside the beds, the paths were shoveled out, then covered with a cloth weed barrier (available through mail order or at garden centers and nursery supply shops). Then, we covered the paths with bark mulch from the sawmill. In your own locale, other waste materials will be readily available to create your pathways, or you might buy them in bulk.

Within each of the larger plots we created five planting beds just under four feet wide and 12 feet long (which is the width of the plot), by laying two-inch by ten-inch rough-cut boards across .

The boards are important. They not only divide the larger beds into manageable sections, but double as pathways. By weeding, cultivating, and harvesting from the boards, we never need to step in the well-dug soil of the planting areas. That way we avoid compacting the soil—not to mention muddy shoes!

Within our kitchen garden are a wide range of microclimates, just as in your garden. Experience shows us we can grow a lot of different kinds of plants, including some we thought we couldn't, as well as stretch the season for quick-growing ones. For example, in early spring our lettuce might grow right against the north stockade, where it can soak up the sun, yet be protected from cold winds. During the summer it will be planted in the north- or west-side shade of the picket fence or under the apple tree.

Because the design of our garden is modular, spun-fabric row coverings and cloches (glass, plastic, or fiberglass devices that trap the sun's warmth and retain it for nighttime protection) can be rigged easily to nurture heat-loving vegetables–like eggplants—throughout our crisp, cool summers, while at the same time provide protection from pests.

The modular design also makes it easy to rotate our crops. This helps to maintain the ability of the soil to keep producing healthy plants, and deter soil-borne pests. Of the four main vegetable plots, each season one is planted to salad greens, onion family plants and such other space-intensive leafy crops as spinach. A second bed is planted to fruiting crops like tomatoes, peppers, eggplants, summer squash and cucumbers. The third is planted to legumes like peas and both bush and pole beans, and the fourth plot gets root and stem crops like carrots, beets, new potatoes, celery root and kohlrabi. Every year we rotate these plant groups clockwise. That's our rotation plan in a nutshell.

A Smaller Family Garden (2400 sq. ft.)

This garden is a more modest-sized version of the large family kitchen garden, keeping the main four-square section and the functional perimeter beds. As with the larger version, the main 12-by-20-foot plots are planted as a series of four-foot by 12-foot beds, and rotated among the main crop groups on a regular basis as defined above. The perimeter beds could be planted with perennial vegetable and fruit crops, with herbs, or with edible and cutting flowers.

If the objective is maximum production from a kitchen garden this size, the key would be to concentrate on crops that yield a lot per square foot, like salad and root crops, plus trellised crops that make the most of what little ground they use: tomatoes, cucumbers, beans, peas and, possibly, melons. Well-planned successions can also raise yields considerably.

As you can see in the illustration on the next page, the perimeter beds could

A Smaller Family Garden

2400 sq. ft. garden. *12' by 20' plots are divided by access planks into 4' by 12' beds, which are rotated among the main crop groups.*

Functional perimeter beds. *Even the edges can be planted in vegetables, fruits, herbs and flowers.*

Arbor. *A small picnic table in the arbor allows meals to be served in this beautiful setting.*

Corner fruit bushes. *Depending on your region, you might plant blueberries, dwarf peaches, or dwarf cherries.*

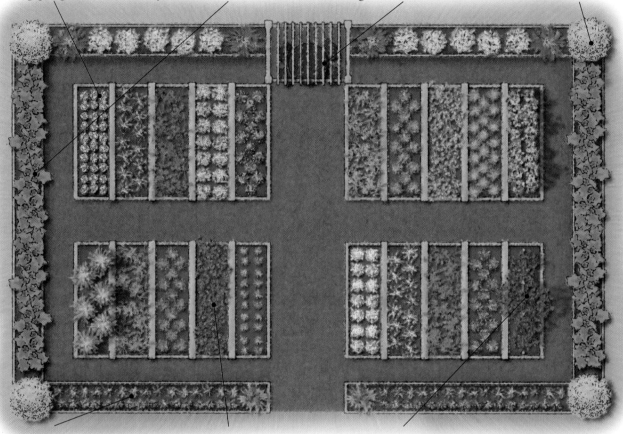

Lower front plantings. *Herbs and strawberries produce well without blocking an enjoyable view in or out of the garden.*

Hedging plants. *Raspberries and asparagus are worth fairly large plantings, to avoid buying this costly produce in the store.*

Trellised crops. *Tomatoes, cucumbers, beans, peas, and melons make the most of what little ground they use.*

Large yields from a small area. *Salad and root crops yield a lot on a square-foot basis, and well-planned successions improve yields, too.*

feature fragrant flowers close to the arbor, with cut flowers filling out the other beds. Along the perimeters are fairly large plantings of raspberries and asparagus, since these are both good hedging plants (not to mention costly crops to buy as produce).

Along the front of the garden, herbs and strawberries produce well without blocking an enjoyable view in or out of the garden. In each corner of the garden is a blueberry bush; other regions might do better with dwarf peaches or cherries, which would be equally attractive.

Any such plan such as the one just desribed is just a model. The choice of plants will be determined by your own wants and needs and those of the family (together with the plants' suitability to local growing conditions). While this kitchen garden is very productive on a square foot basis, it's a beautiful place as well. Imagine when dinner is served on the small picnic table in the arbor. The swallows give way to the bats and tree frogs as dusk settles and the nicotiana flower unleashes its perfume. . . .with a little work this could be yours.

Kitchen Gardening in a Community Garden Plot (750 sq. ft.)

In many towns, community gardens have been established, where you can lease a small plot of land for gardening. For example, the city of Burlington, Vermont, where this movement has been long established, rents out prime river bottom land in fenced plots 25 feet by 30 feet.

A plan for a community garden plot will want to make the most of the space available, so our design breaks up the space into 12 beds, 36 feet square, with

A Community Garden

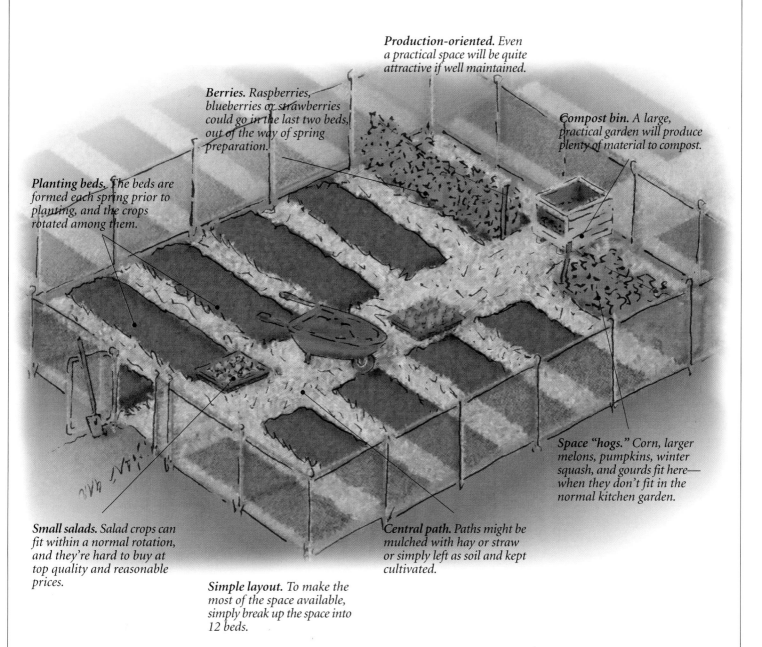

Production-oriented. *Even a practical space will be quite attractive if well maintained.*

Berries. *Raspberries, blueberries or strawberries could go in the last two beds, out of the way of spring preparation.*

Compost bin. *A large, practical garden will produce plenty of material to compost.*

Planting beds. *The beds are formed each spring prior to planting, and the crops rotated among them.*

Space "hogs." *Corn, larger melons, pumpkins, winter squash, and gourds fit here— when they don't fit in the normal kitchen garden.*

Small salads. *Salad crops can fit within a normal rotation, and they're hard to buy at top quality and reasonable prices.*

Central path. *Paths might be mulched with hay or straw or simply left as soil and kept cultivated.*

Simple layout. *To make the most of the space available, simply break up the space into 12 beds.*

a central path leading to a compost bin at the far end. The beds are formed each spring prior to planting, and the crops rotated among them. Paths in a seasonal garden like this might be mulched with hay or straw (or seaweed in a coastal community), or simply left as dirt and kept cultivated.

Desirable crops include small salad greens, which are very hard to get at top quality, and relatively expensive; and raspberries, which are outrageously expensive. Blueberries and strawberries are also expensive, but more likely to be available on a pick-your-own basis. The salad greens can fit within a normal rotation, and the raspberries could go in the last two beds, next to the compost, where they wouldn't be in the way of spring preparation and bed formation. This garden is a production-oriented, practical space, but will be attractive, too, as long as it is well maintained.

A Garden for Two (384 sq. ft.)

If time and space are limited, and the household small—say two people, perhaps young professionals or retired—it's still possible to have a successful, enjoyable kitchen garden. It would be smaller than the two previously described gardens, and it would be designed wisely for low maintenance and, perhaps, a more passive form of involvement. To that end, we have a brick or stone path, wider in relation to the beds for easy, mud-free access, and perimeter beds again. In the center might be a sundial, a birdbath, or a favorite garden ornament.

When space is limited, it makes sense to concentrate on crops that are special favorites of the gardeners, like exotic

A Garden for Two

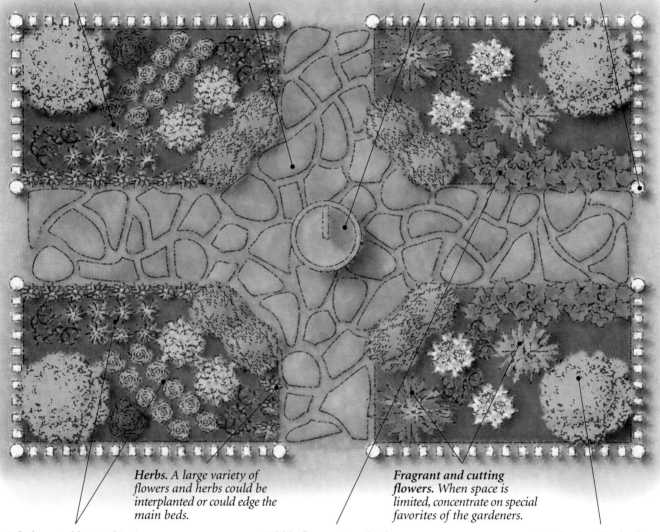

Permanent beds. *Working within defined activity areas makes the garden more beautiful, and the rotation and planting possibilities increase.*

Hard surface path. *For low maintenance and a more passive form of involvement, a brick or stone path permits easy, mud-free access to the beds.*

Ornament. *In the center, where the paths cross, we might find a sundial, birdbath, or a favorite garden ornament.*

Enclosure. *A partly porous fence, such as a picket fence or lattice, allows just enough air through to still air currents while blocking the major force of the wind.*

Herbs. *A large variety of flowers and herbs could be interplanted or could edge the main beds.*

Fragrant and cutting flowers. *When space is limited, concentrate on special favorites of the gardeners.*

Salad vegetables. *In this size garden it may make sense to concentrate on growing primarily those things you want to cook with but simply can't buy locally.*

Edible flowers. *In a kitchen garden, plants like gem marigolds and nasturtiums serve the dual purpose of beauty and food production.*

Fruit bushes. *In the four corners might be blueberries or even trellis-trained currants or gooseberries for visual impact and to make special preserves for Christmas gifts.*

melons on two small trellises at the back, small but productive plantings of mixed salads and edible flowers, or two whole plots of fragrant and cutting flowers. Perhaps herbs edge the central area; in the four corners might be blueberries, or even trellis-trained currants, or gooseberries for visual impact and for making special preserves for Christmas gifts.

This could be a minimalist, perfectionist garden and a source of both pride and relaxation to its stewards.

In this size garden it may make sense to concentrate on growing primarily those things you want to cook with but simply can't buy locally—ethnic specialties like cilantro, shiso, or maybe French "filet" beans, or perhaps "cour-

gettes" (the French name for baby squashes with the flowers still attached). What these are depends on your climate and what you like to eat.

Conversely, if the gardeners have enough time to commit to it, such a garden for two could be the focus of a lot of activity. Instead of the specialty garden described above, it could be an

A Deck/Container Garden

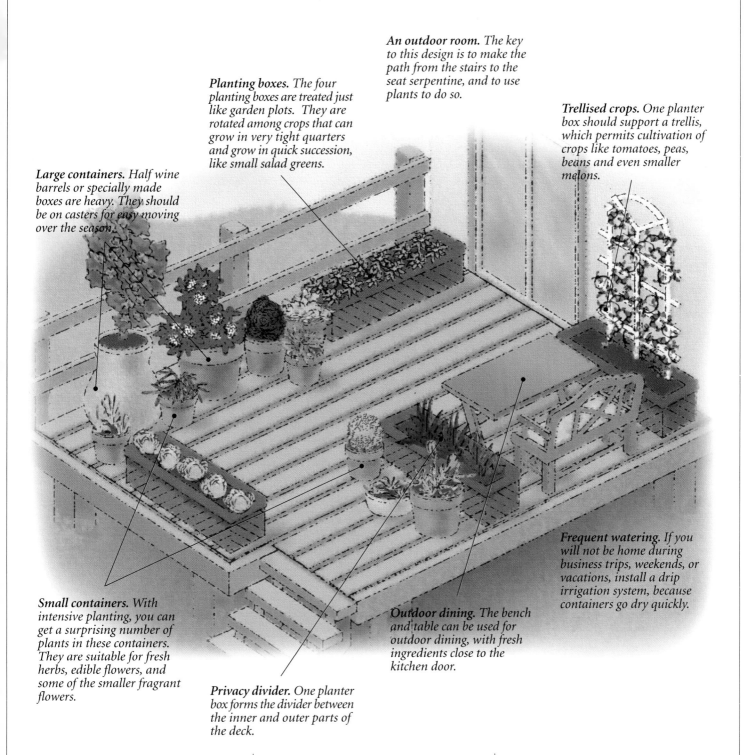

Planting boxes. *The four planting boxes are treated just like garden plots. They are rotated among crops that can grow in very tight quarters and grow in quick succession, like small salad greens.*

An outdoor room. *The key to this design is to make the path from the stairs to the seat serpentine, and to use plants to do so.*

Trellised crops. *One planter box should support a trellis, which permits cultivation of crops like tomatoes, peas, beans and even smaller melons.*

Large containers. *Half wine barrels or specially made boxes are heavy. They should be on casters for easy moving over the season.*

Small containers. *With intensive planting, you can get a surprising number of plants in these containers. They are suitable for fresh herbs, edible flowers, and some of the smaller fragrant flowers.*

Privacy divider. *One planter box forms the divider between the inner and outer parts of the deck.*

Outdoor dining. *The bench and table can be used for outdoor dining, with fresh ingredients close to the kitchen door.*

Frequent watering. *If you will not be home during business trips, weekends, or vacations, install a drip irrigation system, because containers go dry quickly.*

intensive, high-output garden with high raised beds, where fertile soil produces bushels of potatoes, carrots, beets, salad greens, shallots, broccoli, tomatoes, and so forth. A large variety of flowers and herbs could be interplanted or could edge the main beds. Again, what you plant is up to your own needs, wants, and resources.

A Deck/Container Garden (320 sq. ft.)

A kitchen garden may also be a series of plants grown in well-maintained containers or boxes. The main limitation is that container-grown plants need frequent attention. If you are frequently gone on business trips, weekends, or vacations, installation of a drip irriga-

tion system is nearly essential. Even if you ask friends to water everything, remember that they aren't always available when your plants need care, and something inevitably gets overlooked.

With the right design you can grow a surprising amount of food, even in such a small space as this confined garden. More importantly, you can grow some

Opposite Container gardening can bring the joy of vegetable gardening to people who lack space but want to have a few home-grown delicacies.

very interesting food and still enjoy your container-grown kitchen garden as an "outdoor room".

A key element of this design is to use planting boxes in a serpentine pathway from the stairs to the seat. This adds variety and definition to the living areas. The four two-foot by eight-foot planting boxes (each three feet tall) are treated just like garden plots. They are rotated among crops that can grow in very tight quarters and grow in quick succession, like small salad greens, and trellised crops like tomatoes, peas, beans and even smaller melons if you crave them.

The larger round containers—which could be half wine barrels or specially made boxes—can be used to grow larger plants like summer squash (in bush form), eggplants, or if fancy strikes, exotic peppers or heirloom tomatoes. Any large container should be on casters for easy moving over the course of the season to take the best effect of available sunshine (plus, filled with soil as they are, they'll be heavy!).

The smaller containers are suitable for fresh herbs, edible flowers, and some of the smaller fragrant flowers like alyssum or mignonette. With intensive planting, you can get a surprising number of plants in these containers.

Box number two in this model is especially important because it forms the divider between the inner and outer parts of the deck and provides privacy for the bench and table. Overall, this plan creates not just an outdoor space, but also helps you grow a few real delicacies that most urban dwellers rarely have a chance to experience. Nothing beats fresh ingredients close to the kitchen door!

Chapter 3

❦

MASTERING THE BASICS OF KITCHEN GARDENING

Before we talk about caring for plants we need to talk about caring for the soil. It's the soil that feeds the plants. A healthy soil is only about 40 to 45 percent minerals (the part we usually consider soil!). The rest is, by volume, air (about 25 percent); water (about 25 percent); and organic matter (5 to 10 percent), which is the living part of the soil.

The organic matter component is composed of plants, animals, microbes and fungi, along with their decomposing bodies on which others are constantly feeding. Consider nature's endless cycle of decomposition and growth: a double handful of garden soil contains more organisms than there are people on earth! These microbes' incessant activities release the nutrients contained in the mineral segment of the soil for use by the plants. When we

Raised beds make for easy, no-stoop weeding and harvesting.

If you prepare your kitchen garden soil well the first time, it will reward you with many years of superior harvests.

humans consume plant products, we utilize these nutrients.

As long as you put more organic material into the soil of your garden than you take out, you will continue to feed this soil "community", and the soil will continue to improve. Remember, every time you grow a crop you are removing nutrients. Unless you replenish them, eventually your soil will starve, and so will your plants.

The best way to build and maintain soil fertility is to add more organic matter in the form of compost or manure, or to turn under plant wastes or cover crops on a regular (at least yearly) basis.

TESTING YOUR SOIL

The best soil for general kitchen gardening has a pH (an acid-alkaline balance) slightly on the acidic side of neutral—that is, just less than 7.0. If you get your soil tested—and you should, especially when starting a new garden—the report you receive will state the pH of your garden and make a recommendation on how to adjust it toward the optimum. The most common recommendations are: for too acid a soil, add horticultural lime or dolomitic limestone; for too alkaline a soil, add ground sulphur or various sulfates. As with any chemicals, use with care and read the instructions completely. An organic solution is to add lots of sawdust, peat moss, pine needles, leaves, bark or manure. These materials will change your soil's pH more gradually. Again, your extension agent will help you here.

SYNTHETIC VS. NATURAL FERTILIZERS

Some test labs will include recommendations based on adding compost and manure, but most state their recommendations for optimum fertility in terms of the number of pounds of synthetic fertilizer per hundred square feet. You should be aware that synthetic fertilizers supply concentrated nutrients directly to the plants without feeding the soil community. They do not improve the long-term soil fertility, nor its structure. In addition, one-third to one-half of the nutrients never reach the plants. Instead they leach rapidly through the soil, with much of it ending up in our water supply.

In contrast, the apparently low N-P-K analysis of compost and manure (those are the numbers on a bag of fertilizer, denoting levels of nitrogen, phosphorus, and potassium) are a bit misleading in a real-world garden context. They signify *immediately available nutrients*, while most of their nutrient content is tied up in the organic matter, ready to be released slowly, over time—as the plants need them.

Experienced gardeners know the benefits of each type of fertilizer they use, and just how important it is to feed the soil. They also add compost and other organic matter to feed the soil, on an annual basis at the least. In a quick-fix situation you may need to turn to the rapid benefits of a synthetic fertilizer, but remember, your soil is not reaping any benefits from it.

COMPOSTING FOR FERTILITY

Large quantities of uncomposted stable manure are less available these days, but our garden centers have lots of bagged, composted manure that takes its place. In general the most efficient method of building the soil in your kitchen garden is with the addition of plenty of compost: the recycling of plant waste into fertilizer.

Composting is a relatively simple, basic, and natural process, like making bread or building a fire. You take the right ingredients in the proper positions, mix them together, provide a

Carbon/Nitrogen Ratio of Common Compost Materials

Material	C/N Ratio
Grass Clippings	20 to 1
Weeds	19 to 1
Leaves	60 to 1
Paper	170 to 1
Kitchen Scraps	15 to 1
Sawdust	450 to 1
Hen Manure (no litter)	7 to 1
Hen Manure (w/litter)	10 to 1
Straw	100 to 1
Seaweed	25 to 1
Pine Needles	70 to 1
Corn Stalks	60 to 1
Alfalfa Hay	13 to 1

Advance Soil Preparation—The Key to Success

Nothing…*nothing* is more important to the successful growth of plants than proper advance soil preparation. Skip this all-important first step, and you're asking for trouble. Abide by it, and you've taken a huge step in ensuring a thriving, easy-to-care-for kitchen garden.

No matter what type of soil you have, from the lightest sand to the heaviest clay, a liberal addition of organic matter works miracles. Organic matter can be anything from compost to well-rotted leaf mold, fine fir bark or peat moss. Almost every area of the country lays claim to some indigenous, inexpensive organic material, readily available to gardeners for free.

A good rule of thumb is that the amount of organic matter you add should be equal to the depth to which you intend to turn the soil. If you're preparing the soil for raised beds in the kitchen garden, the minimum depth you should till is six inches; eight or 12 inches or more is that much better. This may contradict some traditional advice, but experience has proved it to be very successful.

If you intend to till the soil to a depth of 8 inches, then you should add 8 inches of organic material on top of the soil before you till to incorporate it to the full depth. This takes some doing, but it helps develop an extensive, healthy root system. This results in a hardy, vigorous, productive bed, able to withstand periods of drought, and more resistant to disease and pests.

Depending on what you're planting and the characteristics of your soil, you may want to add fertilizer and lime as you incorporate the organic matter. Explain your situation to your local nursery staff or extension agent to find out if such additions are necessary.

After tilling the organic matter into the soil, rake the area smooth and plant your plants. Build small dikes (roughly the diameter of the root ball) around individual plants, and keep them well watered for the first few weeks after planting. You'll be amazed at the growth the plants put on in such superior soil, even in the first year.

spark, and stand back while nature takes over. Good gardeners never have enough compost!

The fuel for a compost pile is plant waste and its carbon or cellulose content, while the heat is its nitrogen content. The spark is a few shovelsful of soil or compost from another pile, which supplies the living microbes, ready to go to work on the plant waste.

To build a compost pile, simply mix about four or five parts of dry garden waste (shredded corn stalks, leaves, hay, straw, shrub trimmings, etc.—the smaller the pieces, the better for rapid decomposition) with one or two parts green waste (grass clippings, pea vines, etc.) in a pile at least three feet on a side and three feet tall. Sprinkle on a shovelful or two of soil or compost and apply water to the pile until it is moist but not soggy.

Most gardeners prefer to contain a compost heap by constructing or purchasing some kind of bin that allows ample air circulation. Simple lathwork or snow fencing will work, as will hardware cloth (metal netting) or even chicken wire. Plastic or wooden compost

Good gardeners never let leaves or other garden refuse go to waste. Instead, turn it into black gold: compost.

If you get into composting in a big way, you may want to build a series of compost bins for holding compost in various states of decomposition.

containers are available in garden supply stores or by mail.

You can put kitchen scraps (except meat) or fresh manure in the pile, but they are much "hotter" than the green waste and so the proportions of the other materials containing nitrogen will need to be altered downward.

Once you have constructed your compost heap, you have two choices. First, you can just let it rot. After a few days, the pile will heat up. A well-built pile can reach 140°F or more! This lazy man's pile will rot in the course of a year with no attention whatsoever. Just keep building new piles when you have the materials, and after the first year you will have a continuous supply of free, better-than-store-bought fertilizer.

Second, you can increase the speed at which breakdown occurs by forking the pile over to give it more air and re-mix-

ing it, and then letting it reheat. With regular attention it could be fully rotted in a month or two.

Recommendations for application vary, but generally two to four bushels of compost a year per hundred square feet of garden will keep the soil healthy. As an alternative to making your own, in many areas, one can buy compost from municipal composting sites or local commercial sources.

SEEDS VS. SEEDLINGS

Once you have determined the amounts and locations of your various plantings, you will need to decide which are best sown directly in the garden, and which should be started ahead as seedlings or purchased as already-started transplants from your local nursery or garden center.

If you buy already-started seedlings, you will receive plants that are ready to go. In most parts of the country, however, your selection will be limited to the most common varieties, which may not be to the liking of the cook!

PLANT-STARTING EQUIPMENT

It's been our experience that any crop that can be started from transplants, whether started on your own or purchased, probably should be. A trans-

Crops Sorted by Seeding Method					
Seeded Indoors		**Direct Seeded**		**Broadcast Sown**	
Normal	*Possible*	*Normal*	*Possible*	*Normal*	*Possible*
Tomatoes	Melons	Corn	Tomatoes	Salad Greens	Carrots
Eggplants	Beans	Peas	Broccoli	(Mesclun)	Beets
Peppers	Corn	Beans	Cabbage	Cover Crops	Peas
Basil	Beets	Squash	Cauliflower		
Parsley	Squash	Melons	Onions		
Perennial Herbs	Pumpkins	Pumpkins	Leeks		
Cabbage		Spinach	Basil		
Broccoli		Scallions			
Cauliflower		Carrots			
Br. Sprouts		Beets			
Onions		Radishes			
Leeks		Turnips			
Lettuce, early		Kohlrabi			
		Dill			
		Fennel			

Planting day: The best day of the year for many a kitchen gardener.

Timing Chart for Seedlings		
Group 1 (*Start 10–12 weeks before the frost-free date*)	**Group 2** (*Start 6–8 weeks before the frost-free date*)	**Group 3** (*Start 2–4 weeks before the frost-free date*)
Eggplants	Tomatoes	Melons
Peppers	Cabbage	Beans
Parsley	Cauliflower	Br. Spouts
Onions	Broccoli	Squash
Leeks	Lettuce	Lettuce
Perennial Herbs	Endive	Annual Herbs
Celeriac		
Basil		

plant decreases the amount of time a plant needs to be in the garden, and thus makes succession plantings more efficient.

A couple of notes about soil mixes and seed-starting equipment: First, unless you really know what you are doing, you will get better seedlings if you grow them in a commercial potting mix rather than trying to mix your own. These potting mixes are sterile, which is a big help to the young plants because it virtually eliminates the dreaded damping-off disease. If you buy the right kind —it should be brown, not black; very light in weight, and have specks of white and gray (vermiculite or perlite) in it— you will have a lot less trouble getting quality transplants.

My second recommendation is to use some sort of modular growing system like plug trays, not a mish-mash of recycled milk cartons, paper cups and old soup cans with holes punched in the bottom. The key to good seedling growth is consistent treatment, and it's very hard to provide that if you are dealing with all different sizes and types of containers. Numerous well-designed systems are available from mail order seed and supply companies, as well as local garden centers. (See the source listing in Appendix.)

CONTROLLING TEMPERATURE AND LIGHT

Soil temperature is critical for germination. It should average 65° F to 75° F for most varieties (air temperature should be between 70° F and 75° F). Bottom heat, from heating cables or pads placed under the flat, is a good means to achieve this. Another tip: use only tepid water when watering.

Immediately after seeds have germinated, remove any cover you have used and place your seedlings in the light. After the third leaf (or actually the first true leaf) appears, the seedlings should be transplanted to a flat with more space between plants, or better yet, into individual peat pots or other small containers. Try to transplant the seedlings while they are still

The private domain of serious gardeners: A tool shed filled with well-maintained and organized gardening equipment.

small, as they are less susceptible to transplant shock. When transplanting, plant at about the same depth as they were in the flat. Make sure the soil is firmed around the root.

Specifics about sowing seed appear in the next chapter.

In general, try to keep seedlings between 65° F and 75° F during the day time and 55° F to 65° F at night. Give them as much light as possible to avoid leggy transplants. If you're only starting a dozen or so plants, a sunny window will suffice. If you're more ambitious, you can use a number of readily available light sources for this. Garden centers and mail order catalogs are full of different lighting supplies, but lighting requirements needn't be overly sophisticated or expensive.

If there isn't enough light to photosynthesize enough body mass to keep up with the growth rate, the seedlings will become tall and spindly. More fertilizer and more water (or heaven forbid, more heat!) will only make things worse: spindly plants need more light, or less heat, food and water if they are to recover.

Germination and Growing Temperature				
for various vegetable and herb transplants				
Crop	Germ. Temp* (F)	Days to Germ.	Growing Temp (F)	Weeks to Transplant
Tomatoes	60–85	7–14	55–85	6–8
Eggplants	75–90	7–14	65–85	8–10
Peppers	65–95	7–14	65–85	8–10
Cabbage	45–95	4–12	55–75	4–6
Broccoli	45–85	4–12	55–75	4–6
Cauliflower	45–85	4–12	55–75	4–6
Brussels sprouts	45–85	4–12	55–75	4–6
Lettuce	40–80	2–14	55–75	2–4
Basil	65–85	7–14	65–85	8–10
Parsley	50–85	14–28	55–75	10–12
Onions	50–95	7–14	55–75	6–8
Leeks	50–95	7–14	55–75	6–8
Celeriac	60–70	7–14	55–75	10–12

The numbers in this column indicate a range of temperatures where germination will occur for each vegetable crop period. Optimum germination will occur at the midpoint between the two temperature extremes, allowing for some fluctuation between day and night temperatures.

FEEDING YOUR SEEDLINGS

Your seedlings will need to be fed, especially if you're using a commercial potting mix. But remembering when to feed plants can be a problem. We've solved this by using a liquid fertilizer every time we water. We use a fish-based organic fertilizer with seaweed extract added. It provides broad nutrition for the young plants. Our formula is *one quarter* the strength recommended on the label (always read the label first!). This way we don't have to remember when we last fed the seedlings, because we're constantly feeding them.

HARDENING OFF

Once planting time nears, seedlings grown indoors will need "hardening off"—a process by which you adapt your plants from sheltered indoor conditions to the more rigorous requirements of the outdoors.

The necessity of hardening off is apparent when you consider it from a plant's point of view. Plants grown indoors are accustomed to dim light (filtered by windows, even at best), still air, and fairly consistent, controllable temperatures. Once out in the garden they are subjected to bright sun, drying winds, and temperature swings of 30° F to 50° F or more daily!

You can't expect tender plants to adjust to such a different environment overnight. To get your transplants ready

If you grow your own transplants from seed, you'll need a convenient place to do it, preferably out of harm's way.

Recent years have brought a number of innovations for protecting young tender plants from the elements.

Many experienced gardeners favor relatively mild solutions of organic liquid fertilizer applied on a regular basis through the growing season.

hardy plants that can take hard frosts (if they have been hardened off first, as noted above); ❷ the majority of plants that can withstand light frosts only, and ❸ the really tender plants that will be killed or disastrously set back by even a touch of frost.

When to plant

Knowing just when to plant which type of plant is one of the hallmarks of an experienced gardener. It's surprising how many gardeners follow what some people would call folklore. Two ways to gauge the progress of the season are: ❶ to ask experienced local gardeners, or extension horticulturists—they're always ready to tell you just what's likely to happen with the weather—and ❷ to watch the progress of the trees and shrubs in your neighborhood.

For example, despite variations in date from year to year, it is almost always okay to plant your corn and set out tomatoes once the apple trees have dropped the last of their blossoms, or the oak leaves are the size of a squirrel's ear, just as it is safe to plant spinach when the forsythia blooms. Here in USDA Zone 4, carrots sown before the daffodils and the shad trees (*Amelanchier* spp.) finish blooming (about May 10 most years) are likely to be attacked by the carrot rust worm. Plants in the cabbage family (broccoli, brussels sprouts, cabbage, cauliflower, kale, mustard greens, turnips, kohlrabi,

for this change, move them outside to a sheltered location: not too windy, nor too hot or sunny. To avoid a sudden shock, put the transplants on trays and move them about in mild conditions for a bit longer each day. Start by exposing them to outdoor conditions for a few hours per day and work up to leaving them out all day and night. Usually, it will take a week or two before you can set them in the open garden for good.

PLANTING YOUR GARDEN

There are three main groups of plants in terms of planting time: ❶ the few really

	Crops Sorted by Hardiness	
Hardy	Half Hardy (Light Frost)	Tender (No Frost)
Onions	Beets	Basil
Parsnips	Broccoli	Beans
Peas	Brussels Spouts	Corn
Radishes	Cabbage	Cucumbers
Scallions	Carrots	Eggplants
Spinach	Cauliflower	Melons
	Endive	Peppers
	Fennel	Pumpkins
	Kohlrabi	Squahes
	Lettuce	Tomatoes
	Turnips	

Handwritten notes:

6 Anaheim
6 Poblano
6 ...

...depuis +
Ristra for drying

Planting date
approximately
April 12th

N ↓

Seed packets:

Burpee PEPPER — SWEET BANANA

Van... garden ONION SETS — 8 Bulbs — SHALLOTS IMPORTED

Burpee PEPPER — HOT PEPPER MIXTURE

BURPEE HERB — Coriander (Chinese Parsley, Cilantro) — Coriandrum sativum — annual — NET WT 1.7 g — $1.05 — SEED HOUSE COLLECTION

Pencil: DIXON TICONDEROGA 1388 2·5/9

Catalog pages:

SWEET BELL PEPPER

52-617—Park's Whopper Improved Hybrid. A Park High Performer® variety. Our biggest and blockiest main season pepper. Superb quality. Described and illustrated page 5.
(P) Pkt $1.50; 2 Pkts $2.70; 4 Pkts $5.00

56-475—Park's Early Thickset Hybrid. A Park High Performer®. Flavorful and super-productive. Best early bell pepper. See p. 12.
(P) Pkt $1.25; 2 Pkts $2.70; 4 Pkts $5.00

56-540—Purple Belle Hybrid. 75 days. A brand new color to add beauty and excellent taste to salads. So much in demand that leading restaurants have been flying these in from Holland. Attractive, medium sized, 3-4 lobed fruits turn from green to purple, and eventually to red.
(P) Pkt $1.95; 2 Pkts $3.50

52-578—Park's Pot Hybrid. 70 days. Handsome plants, just 10-12 inches tall, bear a heavy crop of delicious crisp, medium size fruits. Exceptionally early and remarkably productive in smaller gardens, pots or hanging baskets, A Park Exclusive. (P) Pkt $1.35; 2 Pkts $2.40

52-655—Golden Summer Hybrid. 67 days. An excellent tasting, very productive golden pepper whose uniform, blocky, mostly 4-lobed bell-shaped fruits start out a very attractive lime green, maturing to rich gold. Fine sweet flavor. The vigorous plants have lush foliage that protects fruit from sunscald. TMV resistant.
(P) Pkt $1.50; 2 Pkts $2.70; 4 Pkts $5.00

52-631—Orobelle Hybrid. 70 days. Our best large-fruited, dark green blocky bell pepper that matures gold. Fruits are 4½ x 4½ inches, with thick walls; excellent at green stage and as giant sweet golden-yellow peppers. The vigorous plants are resistant to PVY. Larger than Golden Bell.
(P) Pkt $1.50...

52-643—Park's Tequila Sunrise. An ornamental pepper with delicious edible fruit 12 to 14-inch plants, 12 inches wide, bear profuse, upright, 4 to 5-inch long fruits, deep green and maturing to warm golden orange. They're delicious and the plants grace the ornamental border, window boxes or pots. A Park Exclusive.
(P) Pkt 95¢; 2 Pkts $1.70

56-451—Gypsy Hybrid. 1981 All America Selection Winner, 62 days. Extremely early and prolific, widely adapted for salads and cooking. Flesh is crisp, sweet and tasty, pendant fruits are wedge shaped, 3-lobed and 3 to 4 inches long. At early maturity they are greenish-yellow, when fully ripe, orange-red. As many as 18 peppers ripen at once on compact 20-inch plants.
(P) Pkt $1.50; 2 Pkts $2.70; 4 Pkts $5.00

56-487—Sweet Pickle. A real double winner! Hand-some as an ornamental bedding plant 12 to 15 inches tall, covered with dense clusters of two inch oval fruits that present a kaleidoscope of bright color — yellow, orange, red and purple, all on the plant at the same time. And the fruit is thick-walled, sweet and tasty. Perfect for pickled peppers, in green and red stages. Perfect for pickled peppers. Starts to mature in 65 days. Illustrated page 115. Pkt is 50 seeds.
(P) Pkt $1.00; 2 Pkts $1.80; 4 Pkts $3.40

52-629—Pimiento Select. Small, mild, smooth, red...

PARSNIP

52-201—Hollow Crown. 100 days. A delicious early vegetable. Sow in rows in spring or summer, and let remain in ground, since Parsnips...

52-354—Cayenne Long Red Slim. 72 days, drying or canning.

52-580—Cayenne Large Red Thick. 75 days. An abundance of medium thick, 6 to 7 inch hot peppers are produced on strong 24 inch plants.

52-566—Hungarian Yellow Wax. 65 days. 6 in.

52-592—Jalapeno M. 73 days. Continuous production of pungent 3½ inch fruit on 26 inch plants.

52-720—Hot Mixture. A well-blended mix.
Above Hot Peppers, each: (P) Pkt 95¢; 2 Pkts 85¢ each; 4 Pkts 80¢ each

52-706—Anaheim TMR 23. 74 days. Relatively mild, smooth, flat 2- chili and tacos. celled pods 8 inches long and 2½ inches in dia-meter. Erect, sturdy plants, 28 to 34 in. tall with good foliage cover to protect fruit from sunburn.
(P) Pkt 95¢; 2 Pkts $1.70

56-437—Thai Hot. If the hot peppers that you've had aren't hot enough, try this one. We've never tasted a hotter, zestier pepper, and we've tried quite a few. Widely used in Oriental dishes, this exotic from Thailand will add a new dimension to your cooking. And the mound-shaped, eight inch plants, covered with one inch peppers in green and red, held upright like little Christmas tree lights, make fine ornamentals, particularly in patio containers and even in hanging baskets. A Park Exclusive.
(P) Pkt $1.25; 2 Pkts $2.20; 4 Pkts $4.00

Photo captions: Purple Belle Hybrid — Thick and Tasty — Home grown peppers — Cayenne Long Red Slim — Super Chili Hybrid

*K*itchen gardening, particularly when space is limited, requires good advance planning.

etc.) set out before the apple trees first show color (usually May 20 or so) are sure to be attacked by the cabbage root maggot, unless otherwise protected. While not infallible, these rules are as good as any when dealing with the capricious ways of weather.

Preparing the soil

The second condition necessary for planting is the state of the soil at planting time, especially early in the season. Make no mistake: working the soil when wet can cause almost permanent damage to its structure—for even 20 years or more! It is imperative to wait until the soil has dried out enough.

There is an easy way to tell when the soil is ready to plant. Take a handful of soil and squeeze it into a ball with one hand; if water appears between the outsides of your fingers, it is too wet to plant. Unfurl your fingers; if the lines of your palm are just visible; and the ball holds together until you nudge it, then falls apart; soil moisture is ideal. Later in the season, the ball may not hold together at all when you open your hand. That means the soil is too dry, and you should water before, and/or after, planting.

Transplanting

Whenever you transplant seedlings, remember these points:

❶ Use only healthy, compact (not spindly) plants.
❷ Prepare and water the soil ahead of time.
❸ Immediately protect plantings from heat, wind, and pests.
❹ Avoid plants with lots of flowers already blooming (they'll drop their blooms shortly after transplanting and you'll have to wait for a new flush of blooms).
❺ Transplants with their roots bound in knots will suffer before their roots spread out (if they ever do).

If you transplant in the evening or on an overcast day, the plants can get established with less stress. If it's hot, set up a simple sunshade of lath, burlap or plywood for a day or two. Where birds are a problem (they especially love lettuce), cover the newly planted transplants with spun-bonded fabric or bird netting, weighted and buried at the edges.

If you plant from flats, *pull* the plants gently apart, since cutting removes roots. Pulling spreads them for quicker rooting. Don't squeeze the soil or you'll compact it and trap roots inside.

Before you are ready to remove plants in packs or containers, water them so the soil won't be dry and crumbly when removed from the container. Do this far enough ahead of time that the water drains away, leaving the soil around the young plants moist, but not wet.

Snip off any coiled bottom roots and gently comb side roots with a kitchen fork to direct them outwards. Then set the plants into their planting holes and firm the soil gently to remove air pockets. Water as needed.

Some plants thrive better with special treatment. Tomato, pepper, eggplant and cabbage seedlings, for example, should be buried to the first set of leaves. They will root along the buried stem. In general, other plants should be planted at the same depth as they were in their original container.

Hex-spacing for highest yields

Your garden will not only be more attractive but more efficient and higher yielding if you set the transplants in what is known as "hex-spacing" at the distances listed in the next chapter for each plant. To do this, don't think of them so much as being in rows, but in grids that run diagonally across the bed, the way an orchard is arranged.

The easiest way to visualize this is to take ten pennies and arrange them on a table so that you have a row of three, then a row of two, nested up against the first three, then three more, and two more nested against this second three. When you consider that plants are more round than they are square, this arrangement makes sense, and it fits the most plants into the least space.

It also saves water and labor because as the plants grow they close over all the space between them, creating a "living mulch", which deprives weeds of the light they need to grow. Another benefit: plants grown closer together shade the soil from the sun, thus retaining soil moisture.

Direct Seeding

Crops that don't transplant well should be sown from seed directly in the garden. This is easy enough if you prepare the

If possible, choose a cloudy day for transplanting plants, or do it in the evening.

garden properly ahead of time, but even the best of gardeners has experienced failure in direct seeding, now and then.

The beginning gardener sometimes kills with kindness. Don't overdo the preparation of a seedbed. If you rake the soil until it's as fine as dust, you'll make mud pies when you water, and your seed will be imprisoned in a tight crust when the soil dries out.

If your soil contains heavy clay, and you don't have time to improve the entire bed, for the purposes of better germination, you can simply add compost or other fine organic material to the area to be planted, specifically to the row or seedbed.

Don't rush the season. With many seeds, there's a fine line between rooting and rotting in cold soil. This is especially true with beans and corn. With such seeds, the warmer the soil, the better the germination rate.

Proper sowing depth is listed in the next chapter, but there's an old rule of thumb that works well. Set the seed three to four times its diameter beneath the surface. For oblong seeds use the shortest dimension instead of diameter. In wet weather or in heavier soils, plant shallower; in drier weather or sandier soils, plant deeper.

Several crops—parsnips, carrots, parsley, cress, and to degree, lettuce—benefit by very shallow planting: one-quarter inch or less. Such shallower planting with a longer germination period calls for close attention to careful and regular watering to prevent the soil surface from drying and crusting.

To address this problem, there are many alternatives. Some gardeners cover soil rows with burlap sacks and water them as needed. Just don't forget to remove the sacks as the seedlings emerge! Alternatively, a one-eighth-inch mulch of vermiculite, very fine bark, or sawdust can prevent crusting and reduce the frequency of watering newly-seeded beds.

Some gardeners sow small seeds in groups of two to six with a few inches between groups. It's said that the seeds help each other up when the soil is likely to crust over, and it gives insurance against seed failures. There seems to be some merit in this method. Just be sure to thin all but the strongest one or two seedlings in each group, or they'll be overcrowded.

When you make a furrow using a hoe, a stick, or even your finger, place a tag or marker at the end. After the row is marked arrange the seeds in the bottom; once you have sown all the rows you intend to, fill in the furrows and tamp the soil lightly. By waiting to cover all the rows at once there is less chance of confusion and an empty or mislabeled row.

Providing support

Any plant that has a vining or sprawling habit, like tomatoes, cucumbers, pole beans, melons or peas, can be given extra

Any vining plant such as pole beans, cucumbers, or tomatoes will take up far less room if they are trained onto ornamental trellises.

space by building a trellis, thereby making use of vertical (air) space as well as horizontal (ground) space.

Trellises actually play a triple role in the garden: ❶ they increase yields per square foot by using the vertical space of the garden to its fullest; ❷ they help control pests and diseases by getting foliage and fruits up off the ground where they are less subject to attack from animals and microbes (which can cause rot); and ❸ if planned and designed with a keen eye, they add important visual interest to the design of the garden.

Numerous materials can be used for trellising. Rough-cut poles make ideal uprights, as does bamboo. Brush trimmings, especially from pliable plants like young willows, can be woven into all kinds of rustic or aesthetic forms, from small trellises to large pergolas. Even such everyday, commercially available materials as finished lumber and chicken wire can be attractive enough, once they're covered with plants.

At the most efficient and high-tech end of the spectrum are ingeniously designed portable, collapsible trellising systems, some of which even have built-in irrigation. These are available from mail order equipment suppliers and garden centers.

Our favorite trellis is a combination of bamboo and untreated hemp or jute garden twine, which can be rigged up in many different configurations, depending on the need of the crop and our design preference. Bamboo is a natural, renewable and aesthetically pleasing material. With just three or four different sizes—four-foot, six-foot and eight-foot lengths—it's possible to design an almost infinite number of different trellis structures. Untreated twine is a plus, because when the end of the season comes, it's a snap to take apart. Just cut the twine off the bamboo and throw the plants and twine on the compost pile to rot. Save the reusable bamboo poles for next year's garden.

MAINTAINING THE GARDEN

Once your plants are in the garden, your care consists primarily of ❶ making sure they have the nutrients, water and space to grow and ❷ protecting them from pests and marauders. If you have built a rich soil, no attention need be given to special nutrients on a regular basis. If you do spot signs of poor nutrition, though, a mid-season feeding may be prudent. We use a commercially-available, fish-and-seaweed-based liquid fertilizer in our garden, and follow the label instructions for "side dressing".

Watering and irrigation equipment

Quick, unhindered growth is the key to juicy, tender, flavorful crops. Most garden plants need about an inch of water a week to grow quickly. Most fruiting plants need ample water when fruits are forming, but will taste best if water is withheld somewhat during fruit ripening, so that the natural flavor elements of the fruits become concentrated.

If your garden doesn't require watering on a daily basis, you can probably get by with hand-watering.

Where summer rains are scarce, a permanent irrigation system is the easiest solution for watering the garden.

Hard to do but necessary, be sure to thin crops to their proper spacing.

You can keep track of water amounts with an inexpensive plastic rain gauge. If rain doesn't provide enough water regularly, you will need to irrigate.

In some areas, where water is plentiful, overhead sprinkling with hoses is a common practice. The problem with overhead irrigation, besides the wasteful loss of moisture into the air, is that frequent wetting of plant leaves provides ideal conditions for the growth of bacterial and fungal diseases. For these reasons, overhead watering is inferior to drip or ooze irrigation, where water is applied directly to the ground.

Huge advances have been made in the past decade in drip and ooze irrigation. Many kits are readily available in garden centers and by mail. Such a watering system can result in great savings of both time and water. As good as they are, though, they must be installed and used right. Talk to the people who sell them and to people who have installed them in their gardens. Get all the information you can about the benefits and pitfalls of each type of system. Again, a step like this requires planning, and any irrigation scheme must be integral to your garden design.

Drip irrigation is made from plastic tubing which has "emitters" placed every so often along its length, each of which allows a metered amount of water (e.g., one-half gallon per hour) to escape. When set up right, drip systems water with no waste and no wetting of the foliage. This is an excellent system for crops that have been transplanted or sown in hills at wider spacing.

Ooze tubing differs in that it is porous along its entire length, and "leaks" at a controlled rate, too, delivering a precise amount of water at a rate that allows the ground to soak it up without puddling. This kind of tubing works better for closely planted crops.

Thinning your plants

Every plant needs a given amount of space to reach its ultimate growth. Thinning is crucial to spacing plants well. If possible, thin by *cutting* plants off rather than pulling them. That way, the roots of the remaining plants won't be disturbed. For specific spacing information, see the Kitchen Garden Plant Guide starting on page 60.

Controlling weeds

Weeds must be controlled, even in the most casual of gardens. A few quick tips will help you keep them within bounds.

First, use the right kind of hoe. My favorite kind is called a stirrup hoe. Instead of a simple flat blade, it has a thin, sharp metal "stirrup," mounted on a swivel, that pivots as you pull it towards you, skimming along just below the surface of the soil, cutting off small weeds at the crown. The conventional American broad hoe, with its wide square blade, is a chopping tool, and suitable, to my mind, only for hilling potatoes and hacking down overgrown weeds. Others use a "Dutch" hoe, which has sharp edges on a triangular cutting blade.

Second, when you cultivate the soil in spring or after a crop is harvested, wait several days before planting. Before you

The bane of every gardener is weeds. If you catch them while they are small, you will cut the job in half.

do, run a hoe across it first and you will take out the first "crop" of weeds that germinated because their seeds were brought up near the surface. From then on, do only shallow cultivation using the stirrup hoe. This by itself will decrease the number of weeds significantly.

Third, keep in mind the old saying about "a stitch in time": Don't wait until the weeds become a problem before cultivating. We make our first pass through the garden the moment the first sprouts of the crop plants appear. Weeds are sure to have germinated within the same time, and they are easiest to remove when they're young.

Mulching

Some widely spaced plants, such as peppers and eggplants, are better mulched than cultivated. And some special crops, like potatoes, prefer a cool soil, even in the middle of summer. For all of these, we use a six- to eight-inch deep mulch of hay or straw (whatever is cheap and available). Cultivate and allow the soil to

After the soil has thoroughly warmed, an application of organic mulch will reduce competition from weeds, moderate the soil temperature, and protect vegetables from soil-borne diseases.

dry for one sunny day before applying the mulch, so that any weeds that have just germinated have time to wither and die. And remember, as a rule of thumb, to wait until the soil has thoroughly warmed before adding a mulch. A thick mulch applied too early (especially around heat-loving plants) will delay growth and maturity.

There are advantages to mulch beyond just weed control. A thick mulch moderates both soil moisture and temperature and also prevents soil bacteria from splashing up onto the foliage of susceptible plants. Many organic materials used as summer mulches are also excellent soil conditioners, when they are tilled backed into the soil at the end of the growing season.

One disadvantage to mulches, however, is that many mulch materials provide an ideal place for slugs to hide. Don't mulch crops like lettuce which are very attractive to slugs in the first place. (A slug tip: These soft-bodied pests don't like rough surfaces, so sharped-edged powders like diatomaceous earth [found at garden centers], spread near mulchless plants, will help thwart slugs. You need to reapply it after rain or watering washes it away.)

Also remember that some mulches and soil amendments are acid in reac-

New products, such as this synthetic spun cloth, are remarkably effective at keeping insect predators at bay.

They often prefer ripening fruits, but in some parts of the country, they'll eat newly planted seeds. They can be discouraged with netting over the crops. It's usually sold in 20-foot by 20-foot sheets and is available at garden centers, nurseries, or mail order companies.

You'll likely need some sort of support or frame on which to hang the netting. With fruits, this might be the trellis itself, but for bed crops, it can be something as simple as wire metal hoops stuck in the ground over the planting bed.

The most adaptable barrier we have used is lightweight, spunbonded, synthetic row covers often used for frost protection. Available under trade names like Reemay, Agryl, or Agrofabric, these covers come in various widths and lengths. We simply drape them over the plant or row and pin the edges or weight them to the soil. No supports are necessary; any slack should be left in the center, as the fabric is so light that, when the plants grow, they will lift it.

Most of these fabrics admit 75 to 85 percent of the available light; protect plants from cold (you can expect plants to endure temperatures four to five degrees colder than their normal tolerance); and are solid enough to prevent the entrance of any insect that doesn't emerge from the soil. Because they're so effective, be sure to remove the covers at flowering time on any plants that need pollination to yield well—not even bees can get in!

Picking pests off your plants

While primitive, simply picking pests off of your plants still works. My grandfather hired me to swat adult cabbage butterflies for a nickel apiece with an old tennis racket. He had many fewer cabbage worms as a result. I pay my own kids a nickel for each adult Colorado potato beetle they kill, and another nickel for every cluster of eggs they crush.

Aphids can be swept off plants with a blast of water from a hose, and Japanese beetles knocked from plant leaves on

tion; some are neutral. Good gardeners find out their soil's pH and use mulches and other soil amendments accordingly. Consult your county extension agent if you are unsure.

CONTROLLING PESTS

There are three ways to control pests, whether they're as small as an aphid or as big as the neighbor's dog (or bigger — like deer!):

❶ prevent the pest from getting to the plants in the first place;
❷ physically remove the pest from the plants; or
❸ kill the pests with some sort of treatment (not recommended for the neighbor's dog!).

Creating barriers

To keep out the large pests, fence the garden. Birds can be a problem too.

A well-designed kitchen garden makes it easy to design permanent, portable methods of protecting crops from birds and other predators.

You're never too young to enjoy the pleasures of a kitchen garden.

cool mornings, when they are sluggish, into a pail half full of soapy water. Slugs, parsley worms and tomato hornworms, to name a few, can be picked off the plants and—steel yourself—crushed underfoot.

Using natural controls

Pests too numerous or too small to remove physically can, as a last resort, be destroyed by dusts and sprays. We use only products derived from natural plant sources, which—though they may be just as toxic as some of the synthetic kinds in the near term—break down more quickly and into more benign compounds than the high-tech types.

The two products which use naturally occurring, active ingredients, and which historically had the broadest spectrum of effectiveness, were rotenone and pyrethrum. Recently, these have been surpassed by an even more effective plant poison extracted from the tropical neem tree.

Despite their natural sources, however, such sprays should still be used only as a last resort. Gardens are highly tuned, well-balanced systems, and if you step in and kill off a portion of the life in a garden, many predator-prey relation-

ships will be disturbed. The system may careen out of balance, possibly requiring further—and usually more drastic—action to preserve the harvest.

Therefore, broad spectrum controls—whether pesticidal or herbicidal, natural or synthetic—should be used only on a spot basis to treat specific plants that are infested. If possible, you should apply them directly to the spot where the pests are present. This way, damage to beneficial organisms is avoided.

Furthermore, you should wear protective gear whenever you use any kind of pest control, because (and I can state this from personal experience) even the most benign of organic poisons can hurt you. Wear gloves and a face mask, then wash your clothes after applying any pesticide. And, as with any chemical product—pesticide, herbicide, fungicide—it's absolutely essential that you read and follow all label directions.

HARVESTING YOUR BOUNTY

Knowing when to harvest for peak flavor is one of the primary skills of the accomplished kitchen gardener. How disappointing it would be to grow your plants

Introducing children to gardening at an early age is one of the best gifts any adult can give.

The author's own garden at apple blossom time. Violas and grape hyacinths add ornamental appeal to this high-production garden. Note the mulched walkways and the framed planting beds.

So-called baby vegetables were all the rage some years ago, and still are in some areas. The name itself is pure hype, an easy way to sell a crop at a high price. In most cases any gardener can grow a baby vegetable simply by harvesting it at the right time. The one thing to remember, though, is that "baby" is not in and of itself necessarily good to eat. Many vegetables, if harvested too young, have no flavor (or worse, bad flavor) and may have poor coloring as well. They may not have had time to develop their unique characteristics.

steadily to maturity, protect and nurse them to peak perfection, and then harvest them either too soon or too late. Each crop has its own schedule and its own characteristics, but they do fall into a few recognizable groups based on the crop type. Those which do not fall easily into one of these groups have their own recommendations in the next chapter.

Harvesting fruiting vegetables

Most fruiting vegetables, such as tomatoes, peppers, eggplants, squash, cucumbers, and tomatillos, can technically be harvested at any time. In fact, summer squashes are ideal when picked young, while the flower is still attached. Peppers are frequently harvested young,

but the piquancy of green peppers is directly related to their age; as they mature, the flavor mellows until they reach the ripe, sweet stage. Cucumbers, unfortunately, develop tough skins and large seeds at maturity, and so should be harvested at the stage when the spines first disappear, unless you want to make pickles, for which they can be harvested even younger. Eggplants can be picked young or allowed to mature, but like cucumbers should be harvested before they show any yellow or golden color undertones.

Harvesting crops with pods

Vegetables that bear pods—peas and beans, primarily—can be harvested at

any time, but the very youngest yellow or purple beans may not have colored up very well. Flavor rarely develops before the seeds begin to swell. There is a good, if subtle, way to tell when this is happening. Look closely at the seam of the pods and you'll notice that one day it stops being convex and becomes concave. At that point, bean pods will have the best combination of flavor and texture.

The same is true for peas. Their seeds will be at the peak of perfection at the convex-to-concave stage. Another clue with peas is that the pods become matte instead of shiny.

Harvesting root crops

Root crops—carrots, beets, turnips, radishes, parsnips, for example—signal their readiness for harvest in a way that's easy to observe. When they first push their crowns through the surface of the soil so that you can see them, they are ready for harvest as "babies," if that's the way you like them. (See the sidebar about the pros and cons of baby vegetables.)

At that stage, it makes sense to harvest in the process of thinning and then

Be sure to include some flowers in your kitchen garden—they're food for the soul.

If you've never experienced a salad made of greens fresh from the garden, you don't know what you're missing.

Finally, buried treasure sees the light of day.

hill soil back up over the shoulders of the remaining plants to keep them in the dark so they stay tender (direct sunlight makes the skins tougher). A few weeks or so later, you will notice that the lowest leaves of the plants no longer point upward, but have dropped nearly parallel to the ground. This is a sign that they have reached ideal maturity at full size.

From that point they may hold well in the garden, but quality is not likely to improve further. If the weather is hot and dry (summer), or hard frost threatens (fall), they should be dug and stored as soon as possible rather than left in the ground. Exceptions to this rule are carrots and parsnips, which store well in the ground for months in some climates. See the next chapter for specific information on this.

EXTENDING THE HARVEST

If you want to store your harvest once the season is past, a root cellar or pantry is the way to go. These storage areas need not be fancy, only arranged so that the crops have good conditions to maintain their flavor and nutrition.

Storing the harvest indoors

While every crop has an ideal set of storage conditions, in general, there are really only two kinds of storage spaces necessary for the vast majority of crops: ❶ a pantry, which is cool, *dry* and dark; and ❷ a root cellar, which is cool, *moist* and dark.

The pantry is for fruiting crops (those that store well at all, like winter squashes, pumpkins and certain kinds of tomatoes; onions, garlic, shallots and the like—not to mention all the canned,

Colorful reminders of the harvest season: This collection of winter squash not only makes a beautiful display, but will provide many meals for cold winter evenings.

Opposite These prizes from the garden are beautiful and last long enough to give us holiday presents.

preserved and pickled harvest). The root cellar is for leaf and root crops (with the exception of onion family crops).

A windowless pantry will do fine for cool, dry storage. For moist storage, the traditional solution is an unheated basement room or perhaps a cool part of the garage. The ideal conditions are 35° F to 40° F and 95 percent humidity, which is cooler and moister than most basements because there's usually a furnace which keeps the basement too warm, or sometimes a concrete floor with a vapor barrier beneath.

If you plan to store a lot of produce, you might consider building an insulated partition so that your storage room is protected from the heat of the furnace. If it is against an outside foundation wall, it will cool down nicely in most cases. If you need more air, you might put a small pipe through the wall or use a small fan.

In some climates you can adjust the humidity by putting a five-gallon plastic pail full of water in the room without a lid. The water in the pail will evaporate and keep things more moist.

Storing the harvest in the garden

The other way to extend the season for home grown food is in the garden. The same floating row covers mentioned under pest control also protect from frost, and can be used to grow crops beyond the normal season. South of the Mason-Dixon line, many of the crops listed as hardy will survive the entire winter with no more protection than floating row covers. Many of the half-hardy crops, sown in late summer for fall harvest, will survive until the temperature drops down to the low teens.

However, don't expect much growth

Herb vinegars are one of the easiest ways to preserve the special flavors of your home-grown herb garden.

from plants once the days get short and soil temperature drops—that's not the point. Whatever plant is ready to harvest, at the time you add the cover, will stay in fairly good shape through most of the winter.

Chapter 4

KITCHEN GARDEN PLANT GUIDE

One of the best things about having a kitchen garden is the freedom it gives the gardener to plant whatever variety of plant he or she wants to try. And lucky for today's home gardeners, there is an almost unbelievable selection of varieties available, especially in the vegetable category. New varieties, old varieties, heirloom varieties, little known varieties from Europe and Asia—you name it, and you can plant it. For the person who likes to cook, it's like having a gourmet produce market in your own backyard. For some of the more unusual varieties, gardeners typically rely on speciality mail order seed catalogs, but even local nurseries and garden centers are expanding their selections of varieties to include a good variety of unusual or hard-to-find plants. As you read through the following chapter, by all means please be tempted to try some of the varieties which may be new to you—you're in for some real taste treats!

There's nothing like fresh ingredients from your kitchen garden to make delicious ratatouille.

a

Artichokes

COMMON NAME
Globe Artichoke

BOTANICAL NAME
Cynara scolymus

RECOMMENDED ZONES (USDA)
See below

This is an ancient vegetable from southern Europe.

The unopened flower buds are steamed or boiled to make them tender (about 45 minutes, or until a leaf separates with a gentle pull). Then the leaves can be stuffed, or dipped in lemon butter or any number of other preparations. The hearts can be pickled.

Along the Pacific coast where there are few frosts, but relatively cool growing conditions, artichokes are grown as perennials. They don't begin to bear until their second season, so where summers are very hot, or winters very cold—both of which are fatal—they must be grown as biennials or even annuals.

Mature artichoke plants.

GROWING
Artichokes are greedy feeders, so incorporate plenty of compost, aged manure, or bagged fertilizer at label recommendations. We use a commercial organic fertilizer with a 5-3-4 NPK rating at about half a pound per plant. Perennial plantings, which grow larger, will need multiple applications. Mulch well and don't let the plants dry out.

While you can grow artichokes from seed, cuttings are preferred. In southern climates, sow just after the hottest weather of the summer is past for following spring harvest. In

Artichoke, ready to eat.

northern climates, the secret to success with artichokes is to trick them into thinking that they have been through a winter—a process called vernalization. Start the seeds 12 weeks before the ground can be prepared in spring, and keep the seedlings warm for at least the first six weeks. Then move them to a cold spot, such as a coldframe outside where they can be protected if the tempera-ture drops below 25° F. They will need a minimum of seven to 10 days where the temperature does not rise above 50° F to vernalize, so keep the cold frame off whenever possible.

If you have space for artichokes, you might place them in the back of the border or treat them as a specimen plant.

Where grown as perennials, they are divided every three to four years, with the divisions planted six to eight inches deep, three to four feet apart in the row, with six to eight feet between rows.

HARVESTING
In milder climates, harvest time is late winter through late spring. Plants yield up to 40 buds apiece.

Harvest artichokes before the buds begin to loosen. Cut one-half inch to an inch below the bud.

PROTECTING
Slugs and snails can be a problem when the plants are young but can be

Artichokes are a gourmet treat, especially straight from the garden.

easily controlled in small plantings by hand-picking. Holding off on the mulch until plants size up will also help as slugs love mulch.

CHOOSING THE BEST VARIETIES
Recommended varieties: 'Green Globe'; 'Grand Beurre', 'Violetto', and 'Imperial Star'.

Asparagus

COMMON NAME
Asparagus

BOTANICAL NAME
Asparagus officinalis

RECOMMENDED ZONES (USDA)
All except deep southeastern USA

An ancient riverside plant of the the Mediterranean basin, asparagus was known and used in ancient Egypt, Greece and Rome. The young stems are best eaten when six to eight inches long. Asparagus is delicious when steamed, boiled, or sautéed (see Asparagus Crepes recipe, page 126).

Asparagus cultivation has undergone something of a revolution in the past five to 10 years. Old methods and varieties have been replaced, and new research has proven that this long-lived kitchen garden perennial can be grown in much less time, with much less trouble, than previously known. The new shoots, which appear in spring, are the harvested part.

A bushel of asparagus spears.

Rite of spring: the first asparagus spears emerge from the soil.

Asparagus is a dioecious plant (there are separate male and female plants), and the traditional varieties of the Washington and California, or UC, strains require yearly vigilance to prevent new seedlings from replacing the original, more productive plants in the garden. New, so-called "all male" plants reduce this labor. They also bear more, since the male plants, which don't produce seed, provide more vigorous shoot growth.

GROWING
Before planting, enrich the bed. Well-tended asparagus beds, supplied with the right nutrients, will bear for 20 years or more! A shovelful of compost per crown is ideal. In subsequent years, apply a minimum of an inch of compost or manure to the bed late in fall, after the ferns have fallen or been cut down. Bagged fertilizers, if used, should be applied in spring, and are of little use at planting time. They have little long-term effect because the nutrients all leach out within the current season.

Asparagus can be grown from seed, but a bed is usually established using one-year-old crowns purchased from nurseries, garden centers, or mail order suppliers. Each crown needs one to two square feet. We plant in beds four feet across, and set three rows of

plants, with the crowns eight inches deep and a foot apart in the row. The rows are offset so that plants in adjacent rows enjoy slightly more than a foot apiece. While it was once thought necessary to dig a deep trench for asparagus and wait two years before harvesting, this has been proven wrong by recent research.

HARVESTING
Harvest asparagus in mid-spring, once the shoots have reached six to eight inches, but definitely before the topmost bud begins to spread. Cut at an angle just below the soil surface with a sharp knife so that moisture doesn't sit flat on the cut end. The first spring after planting, you can harvest for three to four weeks; in subsequent years, four to six weeks of cutting will not appreciably hold back production of the ferns (which are the source of the following year's sprouts).

Twenty five crowns will provide enough for fresh use; if you plan to freeze spears for winter use, consider planting 50 to 100. In season you can reap two to five pounds per week from late spring to early summer.

PROTECTING
Major problems with asparagus are rust, crown rot, and the asparagus beetle. The first two are best controlled by

planting resistant varieties. The beetle can be controlled by applications of the biological spray *Bacillus thuringiensis* (Bt) during the growing season, and clearing the bed of ferns before winter to remove overwintering sites of larvae.

CHOOSING THE BEST VARIETIES
Recommended varieties: whichever of the "Jersey" series of *male hybrids* that is most adapted to your area (check with your local garden center). Warmer-climate gardeners might want to try the variety 'California 500', which needs less cool weather.

Beans

COMMON NAMES
Snap bean, shell bean, lima bean

BOTANICAL NAME
Phaseolus vulgaris; P. multiflorus; P. lanatus

RECOMMENDED ZONES (USDA)
See below

For maximum harvest, pick string beans on a regular basis.

Beans are native to Central and South America. They have become staples in almost every culture and cuisine on earth.

Beans provide some of the best eating from the summer garden. They freeze and dry well, and the pole types provide a classic visual element to any kitchen garden design. We eat their seed pods and/or seeds; bean flowers are also useful as garnish.

GROWING
All beans require the same conditions to thrive. Their care differs only slightly from type to type. All actually add nitrogen to the fertility of your garden. They "fix" nitrogen from the air through a symbiotic relationship with the soil-dwelling *Rhizobia* family of bacteria.

Beans are grown from seed, direct-sown in the garden; one to two plants per square foot. Pole beans can be trained on trellises and fences and are quite ornamental, especially those with colored pods.

Bush Snap Beans
The single most important rule to growing bush snap beans was told to me by a Cornell University breeder, known in the field as "the dean of beans". His advice: "Get 'em, get 'em up and get 'em out." (I call it the "3G's Rule.") By this, he meant that snap beans should be grown in succession, given a once-over harvest, then pulled

The classic 'Blue Lake' bean.

'Goldkist' beans.

out of the garden and replanted. That way they are not in the ground long enough to have many problems, and if problems do develop, then a new crop will be along soon enough to replace them.

We follow his advice and plant just enough for a week's use in the kitchen, and we do it every week after the frost-free date. Sow the seed one-half inch to one inch deep, three inches apart in rows 12 to 18 inches apart. Once the seedlings emerge and start their second set of leaves, snip out every other one, leaving one plant every six inches. Five to ten feet of row (that is, 10 to 20 plants a week) will provide more than enough beans for a family of four; if you are planning a party, increase the size of the plantings six to eight weeks ahead of that time, as most bush snap beans mature in 45 to 55 days.

Bush Shelling Beans

The only real cultural difference with shelling beans is that they are allowed to mature, unlike snap beans. This normally takes close to three months, so while you can't plant until after danger of frost in spring, short-season gardeners should be sure to get them into the ground promptly after that.

Seed depth and spacing is the same as for snap beans, but plant the whole crop at once. For fresh shell beans harvest just as soon as the seeds themselves start to pull away from the wall of the pod. You

'Dragon Tongue' beans.

'Triomphe de Farcy' beans.

can tell this by squeezing the pods; if there is a moment of give before you feel the seed inside, then they are ready. Shell and prepare just like you would for peas.

Dry beans for storage should be left on the plants until the pods are fully dry and the beans rattle within. Pull whole plants and hang upside down in a dark, dry place to dry further, then remove the pods and shuck out the beans. This can be made easier by putting the pods in a sheet, then beating it against a wall or fence to break open the pods.

Pole Beans

Pole beans have a number of advantages over bush beans, especially for gardeners with limited space, because they bear over a much longer period than bush beans. This gives a higher overall yield, and in a much smaller space. The beauty of a bean trellis is just an added bonus!

We have tried a number of systems over the years to support pole beans, and have settled on bamboo teepees (though poles or planed lumber will work just as well). Take four poles no more than four inches in diameter, at least eight feet long, and place them at the corners of a square 30 inches on a side. Lean them together and bind the tops with twine, a foot down from the tips. A neat job will only make the garden a more pleasant place to spend time, so don't be in a hurry. Plant four to six seeds an inch deep around the base of each leg; when they have their second leaves, remove all but

'King of the Garden' limas.

the strongest three to four plants. Within a few weeks they will begin to wind round the poles, and in six to eight weeks will cover the teepee with white or lavender flowers, then long pods of green, purple or golden beans.

If you use longer poles and spread them farther apart at the base, you can make a teepee large enough for the children to play in during the dog days of summer, with healthful snacks hanging right from the walls of the teepee!

Pole beans can be harvested for fresh use at any time and should be cooked just like bush beans—that is, just barely.

Lima Beans

Lima beans are a different species, and generally need warmer conditions than regular beans. Don't plant them until the soil has thoroughly warmed—65° F. They require a longer season as well. Even very early varieties aren't ready for 70 to 75 days. Limas are used only as shell and dried beans. Climbing varieties are, again, more productive on a square foot basis, but bear later.

HARVESTING

Harvest beans from mid- to late summer.

For the French delicacy known as *filet* beans, choose an appropriate variety like 'Fin des Bagnols', 'Triumph de Farcy' or 'Nickel' and harvest when the pods are only a quarter inch thick, regardless of length. These baby beans need to be harvested daily for the highest quality and will yield correspond-

$\mathcal{T}$his collection of various beans were all the product of bush-type plants, suprisingly productive when compared to the old-fashioned runner types, especially if you pick them every day or two.

Purple 'Sequoia' string beans are like jewels in the garden.

For fresh use, snap beans should be blanched only lightly before serving—especially the purple ones, which will lose their color if cooked for more than two minutes. For freezing, a minimum of two minutes is needed to kill bacteria and retard spoilage.

Expect one-quarter pound per plant, per picking for bush beans.

PROTECTING

Major pests of beans are the bean beetle and slugs. Neither need be a major problem if you follow the 3G's rule. One more rule for beans is equally important though: Stay out of the bean patch during wet weather. Foliage diseases and other rots can really grab hold of a bean crop during a wet season if you go out in the bean patch when the plants are wet. It is very easy to spread disease by brushing the plants, transferring bacteria and fungal spores as you go, and infecting the whole crop. Don't do it!

CHOOSING THE BEST VARIETIES

Bush Beans

Standard round-podded green varieties include 'Tendercrop', 'Provider' and 'Bush Blue Lake'; the best round podded purple varieties are 'Royal Burgundy', 'Royalty' and 'Purple Queen'. For round yellow beans try 'Golden Rocky', 'Goldkist', or the new 'Soleil'.

Among flat-podded beans the selection is slimmer, but the beans are generally more flavorful; for a green, try 'Bush Romano', bright 'Golden Roma'; for a purple, 'Sequoia'. One of the best flavored beans of all is 'Dragon Tongue', which is pale yellow with purple stripes!

For the French delicacy known as filet beans, choose an appropriate variety like 'Fin des Bagnols', 'Triomphe de Farcy', or 'Nickel'.

Shell beans

For the French flageolets use a variety like 'Chevrier' or its variants. For Italian dishes, grow a 'Cannelloni' type. There are literally hundreds of

ingly less per picking, but equal to standard types overall. Adjust your plantings accordingly.

Standard bush beans, whether round- or flat-podded, green, yellow or purple, should all be harvested just as the pods start to swell with seed. Extensive research has shown that this is the moment when there is the best balance of texture and flavor. While you can harvest over a fairly long

period with bush beans, we use pole beans for that (see below) and do a once-over harvest for our bush beans. It couldn't be easier: just pull the plants, cut the plants off the roots at the base of the stem with a pair of shears and turn the plants upside down. All the beans will hang down and be a "snap" to pick! Throw plants and roots on the compost pile to recycle.

heirloom American dry beans available from specialist catalogs and seed exchanges; some of our favorites are 'Jacob's Cattle', 'Yellow Eye', 'Vermont Cranberry', 'Black Turtle', 'Soldier' beans, and both 'Swedish' and 'Dutch Brown' beans.

Pole beans

The two old standards are 'Kentucky Wonder' and 'Blue Lake'; these days there are a number of variants of both available. Our overall favorites, however are European: 'Dutch Kwintus' is a flat, green podded bean that consistently bears earliest, and holds its flavor and texture for longer than most others; 'Emerite' is a round podded French variety that can be used for *filets* when small, or snap beans once they get a bit larger. 'Trionfo Violetto' is an old Italian heirloom with beautiful lavender flowers framed in purple that bears long purple pods with great flavor; it is superior even to 'Scarlet Runner' beans for ornamental effect.

Lima beans

Good bush varieties to try include 'Fordhook 242', the super early 'Jackson's Wonder', or various forms of the old 'Dixie Butter Pea'. The standard pole types are 'King of the Garden' and the 'Christmas Lima', both of which can reach 10 feet, but are unlikely to bear in northern states. Check your growing season length to see whether you can grow them.

Beets

COMMON NAME
Beet

BOTANICAL NAME
Beta vulgaris

RECOMMENDED ZONES (USDA)
ALL

Domesticated from a wild plant of southern Europe and north African

A rainbow collection of beets.

coasts, beets were originally grown for their leaves. Since around the 15th century, when Central Europeans began using the swollen roots, they have been bred for the sweet, earthy roots. They have long been used as a sugar source and for livestock feed as well as human consumption.

Beets and their relatives—including chard, spinach—are high in vitamin A, calcium, and phosphorus.

Beets are one of the most underappreciated vegetables in American gardens. Along with their close relative, chard (see below), they are also one of the most useful in terms of producing a wealth of healthy, fine tasting food over a long season from a small space. And they are not boring, despite their homely image. While grown for their roots, the greens can be eaten too. But for that you might as well grow chard, a plant that's actually a leafy form of the beet family.

Beets can be baked whole (they're especially sweet this way), boiled, or pickled. See the recipe for Beet and Walnut Salad in the recipe chapter on page 135.

The 'Italian Chioggia' beet.

GROWING
Though technically biennial, beets are grown as half-hardy annuals. Their culture is pretty simple. The best conditions are a nearly neutral, well-drained soil, high in organic matter (but not too much nitrogen, which develops the leaves more than the roots), and regular moisture. A soggy, acid soil will not grow good beets; on

'Burpee's Golden' beet.

Cylindrical 'Formanova' beet.

the other hand, irregular watering encourages woodiness in beets.

Beets are grown from seed, direct-sown in the garden. Plant beets every two or three weeks from mid-spring until about 90 days before the first hard freeze of fall for a continuous crop. Those that mature during very hot weather will not be as tasty as those harvested during more moderate spring and fall weather. However, with prompt attention to watering and a good mulch, they will still be well worth the trouble. In areas where the temperature doesn't drop below about 15° F, beets can be left in the ground all winter with little more protection than a layer of hay or leaves, and harvested as needed.

Sow seed half an inch deep with only about four seeds to the foot. For quicker germination, soak the seeds for a few hours. Space the rows eight to 12 inches apart in beds. Each beet seed is actually a fruit with four to eight seeds in it, so a few are almost certain to come up at each spot. Once they reach a few inches tall, thin the plants to three inches apiece, leaving only the strongest seedling in each spot. As the plants begin to crowd, remove every other plant and use the thinnings for salads or steaming greens.

HARVESTING

You can harvest beets at any time late spring through late fall, but the best quality roots (of all but the storage kinds) are one to three inches in diameter. Use the small ones whole for pickling or boiling; the larger ones can be boiled or baked. Baking preserves the color of red beets, which breaks down after two minutes in boiling water, unless you leave a minimum half inch of top on the whole, unskinned roots.

Large, winter storage beets should be left in the ground until hard frost threatens. Then cut the tops an inch above the crown and store the root, uncleaned, in damp leaves or sand in a root cellar until you use them.

Twenty-five feet of beets will usually be enough for a family.

PROTECTING

Leaf miners can be controlled by timing plantings to take advantage of the miners' inactive periods (usually late spring to early summer). Or, you can cover the bed with floating row cover during that period.

CHOOSING THE BEST VARIETIES

Our favorite beets are the unusual ones. The 'Albino' beet, which is pure white and one of the sweetest available, is ideal for salads as it doesn't bleed and it is a very vigorous grower. 'Burpee's Golden' beet is also very flavorful and has beautiful coloring, but is a weak grower. The heirloom 'Italian Chioggia' beet, also known as 'Bulls-Eye Beet', is perhaps the most unique of all, with a pink skin and concentric light and dark rings in the root!

Among the standard red beets, 'Detroit Dark Red' and its variants are the most common, and some of the hybrids like 'Big Red', 'Red Ace', and 'Pacemaker' are very uniform and productive. Try 'Cylindra' or 'Formanova' for their carrot-like roots that provide consistent one-inch-diameter slices—very handy for making pickles and preserves! 'Early Wonder Tall Top' is bred primarily for greens, but if it is beet greens you want, grow chard.

SPECIAL NOTES

When boiling beets, don't cut up the roots, or they'll "bleed" and turn the water red. Be sure to leave an inch of greens at the top for the same reason.

Broccoli

COMMON NAME
Broccoli

BOTANICAL NAME
Brassica oleracea

RECOMMENDED ZONES (USDA)
ALL

The entire cabbage family, of which broccoli is a prominent member, has been used for millennia in Europe and Asia. Broccoli's specific heritage is from Great Britain and Southern Europe.

Despite the derision of a past president, broccoli has grown in popu-

'Italian Romanesco' broccoli.

larity over the past couple of decades, and deservedly so. It is a fine-tasting and healthful table vegetable, relatively easy to grow and not, as we have found through recent research, greedy for space. The unopened flower buds are used steamed, boiled, or sautéed, or raw in salads or with dips.

See the recipe for Broccoli with Cheese on page 131.

GROWING

This biennial is grown as an annual. In smaller gardens you can grow broccoli in tightly spaced beds, or as specimen plants. Broccoli needs a rich soil and adequate moisture. Hot, dry conditions will not produce good quality heads.

There are essentially three ways to grow broccoli, depending on your desired result: 1) Florets, 2) Heads, and 3) High-intensity.

For all, start with seedlings. The seed should be sown in a one-inch plug about a month before the last hard frost of spring, or, for a fall crop, about 60 days before the weather cools down. The plants can withstand frosts down into the upper 20s without much damage.

There is nothing like the taste of broccoli, fresh from the garden.

'Violet Queen' broccoli.

❶ For a long-lasting harvest of smaller **florets**, set the seedlings 18 to 24 inches apart and a little deeper than they were in the plug. Once the plants have reached two feet tall or so, and the central bud has reached three inches across, harvest it by cutting off an inch below its base. Give the plants a side dressing of available fertilizer—we use a handful of 5-3-4 organic fertilizer. The plants will then produce an abundance of side shoots, and if you continue to harvest the buds at the three-inch stage, the plants will keep producing for quite some time.

❷ If you'd rather grow **large central heads**, follow the same plan, but leave the central bud to use the fertilizer itself. For a real prizewinner, remove any side shoots that start to form; we've got 14- to 18-inch heads of broccoli this way.

❸ For the **highest yield** in a given space, follow a different plan: set seedlings only eight inches apart in a very fertile, well-prepared bed. Crowding will cause the plants to form only a small, central bud, about four to six inches across, but the increased plant density (six times as many plants in the same space!) will almost double the yield per square foot. What's more, the buds will tend to mature all at once, which is ideal for freezing.

HARVESTING

Late spring through late fall; winter in mild climates.

Harvest broccoli while the buds are still tight, but when the individual florets have begun to swell. Even if you aren't ready to use them, cut all the heads that show any yellow so the plants are pushed to produce more.

The stems should be cut on a slant, so water doesn't collect on the cut stem top.

PROTECTING

The pests and diseases of broccoli are shared with most of the other cabbage family crops. The most destructive pests are the root maggot, the cabbage worm, and the cabbage looper.

The root maggot is the larva of a fly that lays its eggs in the soil at the base of the stem. The larvae then burrow into the roots to feed, causing the plants to wilt. The best control by far is to put one of the commercially available spunbonded, floating row covers over the plants as soon as they are set out in the garden. This will prevent the fly from laying its eggs and alleviate the infestation of larvae. Once the apple trees have dropped their blossoms, we've found that this fly's egg-laying season is over and the covers can be removed. Close observation in your own garden should provide similar knowledge of this pest's habits there.

The worm and looper are more difficult to control, because they are present throughout the season. Both can be killed by *Bacillus thuringiensis* (Bt), a bacterial spray that attacks the gut of soft-bodied caterpillars. Available under a number of trade names, Bt is simple to use. Following the label instructions, spray the plants as soon as you notice the first feeding damage: irregular holes in the leaves, and small piles of leaf-colored excrement. Once the pests eat a treated leaf, they stop feeding and die within a few days. If you must water the crop, or it rains, reapply Bt. This schedule must be repeated periodically through the season to control each new hatch.

Cabbage family diseases are primarily soil-borne. The only real control is to be sure that you rotate your plantings so that they aren't in the same plot year after year. We plant broccoli in a given spot only once every four years.

CHOOSING THE BEST VARIETIES

Most of the broccoli in American gardens these days is of hybrid origin. Our favorite varieties are 'Green Comet' (for production of side shoots); and 'Premium Crop' and 'Super Dome' (which produce large heads). There are also some so-called "purple cauliflowers" that could be considered broccoli. The two most common—both of them good varieties—are 'Violet Queen' and 'Burgundy Queen'.

A very interesting form is the 'Italian Romanesco' broccoli, which, if the season is gentle enough, forms elaborate conch-shaped heads of chartreuse with a mild and unique flavor.

Brussels Sprouts

COMMON NAME
Brussels Sprouts

BOTANICAL NAME
Brassica oleracea, Gemmifera group

RECOMMENDED ZONES (USDA)
ALL

Most people have eaten only store-bought or overcooked Brussels sprouts and have little regard for them. This is a shame. Garden-grown Brussels sprouts have an incredible sweet flavor hard to match in any other plant. They're especially good to eat after they undergo a period of cold weather.

Brussels sprouts hail from northern Europe and are in the same family (the *Brassicas*) as broccoli, cabbage, cauliflower, etc. The Brussels sprout is originally a seaside plant, but in gardens it reaches its perfection in cold

Instead of storing Brussels sprouts indoors, some gardeners prefer to let nature take its course, claiming the cold improves flavor.

Mature Brussels sprouts.

climates where temperatures hover in the twenties during the fall.

See the recipe for Brussels Sprouts with Chestnuts on page 135.

GROWING

These biennial plants are treated the same as broccoli, but started a few weeks later and allowed to grow the whole season for fall harvest. There is no point in starting them early as the flavor doesn't develop until after frost. In smaller gardens, they are best grown as specimen plants. They need a minimum of 18 to 24 inches per plant to do well; 24 to 36 inches is better.

HARVESTING

Late fall; winter in mild climates. Harvest one of two ways: for an extended harvest simply break off the small stem-borne heads sequentially up the stalk as they reach an inch or more in diameter. For storage or once-over harvest, cut off the top of the plant four to six weeks before your desired harvest date, preferably after the first frosts. This will cause all the side sprouts to mature at once instead of one after the other. You can either break them off the stem for immediate use, or uproot the plants and put them in a root cellar with some damp sand or leaves heaped over the root ball.

PROTECTING

Pests and diseases are generally the same as with other cabbage family members, although Brussels sprouts are less bothered by them than other brassicas.

CHOOSING THE BEST VARIETIES

As with broccoli, most of the varieties in cultivation are hybrids, and they come in many different maturity ranges. Choose one that is appropriate for the length of your growing season. We use 'Prince Marvel'. One fantastic old open-pollinated variety that is still available from seed exchanges is 'Rubine', the red Brussels sprout. It is best adapted to long-season areas.

SPECIAL NOTES

Start seedlings one month later than other members of the cabbage family, as Brussels sprouts mature best in the cooler temperatures of late fall.

·····

C

·····

Cabbage

COMMON NAME
Cabbage

BOTANICAL NAME
Brassica oleracea

RECOMMENDED ZONES (USDA)
ALL

Cabbage is another unglamorous vegetable that is actually a star performer for kitchen gardens. Home grown, it has much more flavor than the kinds in the market, both because of the varieties used, and how it is grown. Cabbage is used fresh in salads and slaw; steamed, boiled, or pickled.

GROWING

The best tasting cabbages are grown in rich, neutral (near 7.0 pH) soils with the benefit of consistent moisture. If the weather is dry, it is important that they receive extra water; otherwise, their growth will slow and the leaves will toughen. Then, if another wet spell arrives, the heads, unable to expand quickly enough, will split open.

In cooler climate gardens, cabbages can be grown through the season; in warmer climates they grow best—and taste best—in spring and fall. We start transplants three to four weeks before the last hard frost in spring, and set the plants out at that time. If you are using a small variety (which we recommend), set the plants eight to 12 inches apart in beds or borders. Larger varieties, including most of those grown as a fall crop for storage, need 18 to 24 inches apiece. Regular, small plantings will yield a succession of heads perfect for the table. The last planting should be timed to mature after the light frosts of fall, but before the temperature drops below 20° F, or the heads will be damaged.

HARVESTING

Late spring through late fall; winter in milder climates. Yields two to five pounds per plant.

Cabbage can be harvested at any stage until the heads become solid; you'll get better quality by harvesting a little young, instead of waiting.

PROTECTING

Pest and disease problems are essentially the same as for broccoli, and controls are the same as well.

CHOOSING THE BEST VARIETIES

For home use, we recommend growing

Mature cabbage needs space.

Bountiful cabbage harvest.

only the small kinds, especially the pointed-head cabbages like 'Early Jersey Wakefield', an old American heirloom with flavor so good it is still popular after a hundred years. It is also a beautiful plant: Bishop's hat prim-and-proper, growing in a geometric bed. It deserves a spot solely for its beauty, but it tastes great.

Carrots

COMMON NAME
Carrot

BOTANICAL NAME
Daucus carota

RECOMMENDED ZONES (USDA)
ALL

The carrot we know today is a relatively recent invention of the Dutch, who developed it about 400 years ago from the ancient purple and yellow varieties more than twice that old. Carrots originated in Central Asia and the Near East.

A good carrot should have a thin skin and a narrow center core. It should be crisp without being fibrous. It should be sweet! Carrots like that are hard to find anywhere but in your own garden. Carrots have high beta carotene content, a precursor to vitamin A.

Carrots are used raw in salads, slaws, alone; steamed; baked. See the recipe for Carrot Cake on page 134.

GROWING
The best soil for carrots is nearly neutral, very high in organic matter, yet not overly rich in nitrogen. You can attain these conditions (which favor most root crops) by turning in a lot of organic matter in the fall, or growing a cover crop that is turned in once spring arrives. Raised beds are a great idea for growing carrots, as they are with root crops in general. In acid soils, make a yearly fall application of lime to bring pH up close to neutral according to the needs of your soil.

Carrots are grown from seed direct-sown in the garden. For maximum yields, grow carrots mixed with radishes in tightly spaced rows or in an alternative spacing arrangement. If in rows, space the rows eight to 12 inches apart. No matter which you choose, plan on two to three inches between plants.

Sow the seed one-quarter to one-half inch deep in the bed and thin them according to how big you want the plants to grow. Thinning carrots is no fun until they are large enough to eat, yet the seed is small and hard to handle precisely. Many inexperienced gardeners sow too thickly, and then are

'Tochon' carrots.

The short 'Paris Market' carrot.

forced to thin the rows, as tedious a garden chore as was ever invented.

We have a trick to avoid this, however: Mix in some radish seed, or simply sprinkle some in the furrow after seeding carrots, say one radish seed every inch or so. That way, the radishes, which germinate quickly, will loosen the soil for the weaker-sprouting carrots. Later, once they size up, the radishes can be harvested for the table. As you do so, you'll be thinning the carrots, and many of them will be pulled up with the radishes. Those remaining will grow to usable size before needing to be thinned again, and it is not such a bad job if it yields baby carrots to munch! Replant small amounts every couple of weeks to keep your kitchen stocked with young, crisp carrots.

HARVESTING
Late spring through late fall; fall and winter in milder climates.

Harvest carrots for fresh use as soon as they color up; before that point they don't taste like much. Beyond that, we generally like them as young as possible. Late crops (sown six to eight weeks before the first fall frost) can be left in the ground until it freezes solid and will stay in good condition. In all but the most severe climates, a deep mulch will carry them through the winter.

Dutch finger type, 'Minicor'.

PROTECTING
Carrots have relatively few pests. Parsley worms—large dappled yellow and green worms that feed on the foliage—can be hand-picked. The rust fly, whose larva burrows into the roots, is easy controlled with a floating row cover, which need only be kept on during its early spring egg-laying period. In most areas, once the apple trees bloom, they are done laying, and the covers can be removed.

We prefer the smaller types like the Dutch finger carrot 'Minicor', and the heirloom 'French Touchon'.

Cauliflower

COMMON NAME
Cauliflower

BOTANICAL NAME
Brassica oleracea

RECOMMENDED ZONES (USDA)
ALL

In contrast to its *Brassica* cousins, broccoli and cabbage, cauliflower originated in the milder climate of the Mediterranean basin.

Cauliflower is the queen of the cabbage family: more delicate and refined than its siblings, and a bit more difficult to grow well. It's eaten steamed, boiled, and raw in salads and crudites.

In the north it is a spring, or especially, a fall crop, and in the south a winter crop. Only in the coolest climates can you grow a good cauliflower in the summer.

GROWING
Be sure that it has the best soil conditions: neutral pH, high organic matter, and good drainage with adequate moisture.

Start seed as you would for other members of the cabbage family, but don't set the plants out until the weather is settled. Too much cold and it will run to seed instead of

The unusual green cauliflower.

forming the dense white "curds" you are after. Give the plants 18 inches apiece. We set a row of plants down the center of a three-foot-wide bed and use the edges for smaller plants like cabbage.

HARVESTING
Once the white buds or "curds" in the center of the plant reach the size of your fist, either break the rib of the outer leaves so that they layer over the head, or use a rubber band or twine to bind them vertically and shade the center. This will blanch the "curd" and keep it tender, white and tasty. Cut just below the base of the head once it starts to grow out of the cover.

Harvest in summer and early fall in cooler climates; fall and winter in milder climates.

PROTECTING
Pests and their controls are the same as for broccoli.

CHOOSING THE BEST VARIETIES
We grow the long-known hybrid 'Snow Crown', which is widely adapted around the country and relatively resistant to weather fluctuations. (There are also cauliflowers with pale green curds and the so-called purple cauliflowers, which we treat as broccoli, and they are listed there.)

'Snow Crown' cauliflower.

Keeping the cauliflower tender.

Celery & Celeriac

COMMON NAMES
Celery, Celery Root

BOTANICAL NAME
Apium graveolens

RECOMMENDED ZONES (USDA)
Zones 5 to 10

These are ancient medicinal plants known to the Greeks, but not really cultivated for the table until the Middle Ages.

These two close relatives are not widely grown in American gardens for two very opposite reasons. Celery is well-known but considered hard to grow. Celeriac is a popular crop in central and eastern European gardens, grown for its swollen root, but is unsung in America. It is quite easy to grow.

At maturity (four to six inches across), celeriac roots are wonderful parboiled, then sliced crosswise half-an-inch thick, battered and fried (see the recipe for Celeriac Remoulade on page 135). Celery is used raw in crudites, sliced and used for seasoning.

The swollen roots of celeriac.

Celeriac is usually baked or boiled. Celery seed is used as a seasoning. Celery does require more attention and time than most crops, but celeriac requires only the time and is easy to grow. Both can be grown without undue trouble if you follow a few basic needs.

GROWING

As with carrots and beets, a fertile, well-drained soil, not too nitrogenous, is essential. It should contain ample organic matter and hold moisture, but provide good drainage. Another requirement is ample watering, so your soil needs to retain moisture well.

Sow in flats, eight to 12 weeks before the end of frost, and keep warm, as you would for eggplants or peppers. Celery and celeriac are biennials. Thus you must avoid letting these biennials feel they have been through a winter or they will run to seed instead of producing a crop. The tiny seed should be thinly sprinkled on the surface of moistened potting soil and pressed in, then the flats or pots covered with a water-proof cover to hold the moisture high until germination.

Celery needs more room—12 to 18 inches per plant—than celeriac, which will do quite nicely spaced a foot apart.

Once the seedlings have their first true leaves (the serrated ones), thin until each plant is one-quarter to one-half inch separate from its neighbors. When the plants touch, separate them again until, two months later, they stand two inches apart. If necessary transplant to larger quarters.

Celeriac can be set out in the garden as soon as the danger of hard frost or a full week of sub-50° F temperatures is past. Celery, however, should not be set out until all danger of frost is past so that its faster growth rate is not held back.

Celeriac's quality can be improved if the top of the roots are uncovered once

Celery needs a well-drained soil.

they begin to swell and the tiny feeder roots, that spring from their sides, are rubbed off with your finger. This will lead to smoother roots, which clean more easily once in the kitchen. After rubbing, hill soil back around the root crowns to keep them blanched and tender.

Celery needs a bit more attention. The most important thing is to make sure the plants never suffer for water; once in the ground, an inch a week, if not supplied by rain, should be the norm. For the most tender stalks, the plants should be wrapped with cardboard, once they approach full size, and then mulched with hay, leaves or soil to blanch the stalk, and thus temper both flavor and texture.

HARVESTING

Harvest celery any time after the stalks reach usable size, about 90 days after setting out, by cutting the plants off at the soil line with a sharp knife. Celeriac roots should be allowed to reach a minimum of two inches in diameter. If well grown in rich soil, and left for the full season—that is, until the first hard frosts of mid-fall (about 120 days)—they can reach four to six inches across.

PROTECTING

Once set in the garden, celeriac needs little more attention than weeding and an occasional patrol for parsley worms (described under carrots).

Celery: 'Utah' or 'Florida' strains.
Celeriac: 'Alabaster', 'Diamant', or
'Prague' strains.

Chard

COMMON NAMES
Swiss Chard, Leaf Beet, Perpetual
Spinach

BOTANICAL NAME
Beta vulgaris

RECOMMENDED ZONES (USDA)
ALL

There are two general kinds of chard:
those harvested for the leaves, and
those harvested for the stems. Leaf
chard, usually called Leaf Beet or
Perpetual Spinach, is used, if small, for
salads, and if large, steamed or boiled.

Stem chard, usually called Swiss
Chard, is also used for steaming or
boiling, but can also be used as a
substitute for the Chinese cabbage
known as Pac Choi, as the wide, white
stems have a similar texture, and the
plant has a longer season in the garden.

Chard, ready for the soup pot.

Colored varieties are very ornamental
and can be used for edgings.

GROWING
Chard is essentially the same plant as
beets, and in general it needs the same
culture, with a very few differences.
First, succession plantings are not
necessary (though they may still make
sense in long season gardens to
provide young plants for harvest).

'Ruby' Swiss chard.

The plants can be harvested for
individual leaves throughout the
season. Second, because the plants are
usually left in place long enough to
grow quite large, they should be
spaced at least a foot apart, and 18
inches is even better.

HARVESTING
Grown the same as beets, but the
leaves are harvested, singly, over the
course of the summer, fall, and, in
milder climates, winter. Cut the leaves
as needed, leaving the center of the
plant to grow new outer leaves.

PROTECTING
Same as for beets.

CHOOSING THE BEST VARIETIES
Popular leaf chard varieties include
such red varieties as 'Ruby' and
'Charlotte', while green-leaved varieties
may be simply called "Perpetual
Spinach", or have cultivar names, like
'Erbette'.

One widely grown variety of Swiss
or Stem Chard is 'Lucullus'; however,
our favorite is an old, aptly named
Italian strain called 'Monstruoso', or
'Mammoth'.

Young plants of Swiss chard, correctly spaced for best harvest.

Chicory

COMMON NAMES
Chicory, Endive, Escarole, Radicchio, Witloof

BOTANICAL NAMES
Cichorium intybus; Cichorium endivia

RECOMMENDED ZONES (USDA)
ALL

Chicory is an ancient wild plant in Europe and Asia, now widely naturalized in America as well. It has been cultivated since antiquity and is now gaining in popularity.

This is a large and diverse family of plants, closely related to lettuce and more common in American supermarkets, but not widely grown in American gardens. These are treasured crops for Italian-American gardeners.

GROWING

Chicory culture falls into three major categories, based on plant type and growing regimen.

Endive and Escarole (*Cichorium endivia*) are the most lettuce-like of the family. They are grown the same as lettuce, and have much the same season, though they are somewhat hardier. The taste is also more bitter; this

Chicory's attractive blue flowers.

bitterness is usually tempered by blanching.

The best crops of endive and escarole are grown during cool weather: winter in the south; spring and fall in more temperate areas. The seed can be direct-sown as soon as the ground can be worked in spring (or as soon as the weather starts to cool in the deep south), or started in flats a few weeks before that for transplanting after danger of hard frost.° Final spacing in the garden is a foot apiece.

The lettuce-like escarole.

'Fine Curled' endive.

To blanch the heads, gather the leaves in one hand, lift, then slip a rubber band around the tips to hold them tight. Seven to 10 days later, cut at ground level. If heavy rains come, the rubber bands should be removed or the heads may rot.

The most common varieties have relatively broad leaves, like 'Full Heart Batavian' and its variants, but our favorite varieties are almost exclusively the finely-cut leaved varieties known in Europe as *Frisee*; try 'Galia', 'Fine Curled', or 'Salad King', which while not as delicate as some of the others, is extremely disease- and weather-resistant.

The second major kind of chicory belongs to the closely related species, *Cichorium intybus*. These are mostly broad-leaved kinds, and form either squat, round heads, or tall, thin heads a few inches across. So-called **Belgian Endive**, widely available in American

Brilliant red Italian radicchio, slightly bitter, but delicious.

supermarkets, is one of the latter. It is forced from fall-harvested roots placed in cellars, and thus blanched white.

All members of this species can be grown in the same manner: sow direct in the garden 90 to 120 days before hard fall frost, thin to 12 inches apart, and keep weeded, watered and fed. When hard frost threatens in the fall, cut the plants back to an inch above the soil line. Cover with an old pot, or, in cold areas like ours, dig the roots and bring them inside to a place where they can be kept at around 50° F and absolutely dark. They will resprout, and the new heads can be harvested.

While the standard Italian radicchio, which has recently grown in popularity here, can be forced indoors, it is usually specialized Belgian Endive (Witloof) hybrids like 'Zoom', 'Toner', and 'Robin' that are normally used for this, while the older kinds like 'Chiogga', 'Verona', and 'Treviso' are grown outdoors. Some or the latest introductions, like 'Nerone' and 'Augusto' can be grown just like the endives mentioned earlier, and will form heads from spring planting.

The third group is a whole series of **heirloom varieties**, mostly Italian, that are sown direct in the garden in late summer or early fall and then left to go dormant over-winter. Then they resprout as the weather warms again for an early spring harvest. Some of the more common kinds are 'Dentarella' (Italian Dandelion), 'Puntarella' (harvested for its stems, like asparagus), and 'Grumulo' ('Ceriolo'), which forms small, Bibb lettuce-like heads.

Corn

COMMON NAMES
Corn, Sweet Corn, Popcorn

BOTANICAL NAME
Zea mays

RECOMMENDED ZONES (USDA)
ALL

Summer's here! The deservedly popular 'Silver Queen' corn.

Corn, along with potatoes and squash, is one of the New World's major contributions to the world's food crops. Very few people raised in the country don't have memories of shucking out fresh-picked corn next to a steaming kettle of water, and later, gingerly handling the hot ears to roll them in a slab of butter. Along with eating the first ripe tomato, it is one of the quintessential garden experiences. Although a space hog, corn can be grown in the kitchen garden, if you have the room and *really* want to grow it next to the kitchen.

Corn is one crop where it really pays to understand how it grows. Plants have both male (tassels) and female (ear and silk) parts, but they cannot fertilize each other. Thus, pollen from the tassels of one plant must reach the silk of another plant before the kernels (each is connected to a strand of silk!) on that plant will begin to swell and grow. This has two important implications for the corn grower.

First, it means that you must plant your corn in blocks or hills, rather in single rows. This means four rows side by side, even if they must be short, so that no matter from what direction the wind blows, pollen will be spread throughout the planting. Second, since corn is wind-pollinated, it cross-pollinates easily, and some kinds of corn will not produce an edible crop if grown too close to other kinds.

In the last 10 or 20 years, wholly new kinds of sweet corn have been developed that not only have greatly enhanced sweetness, but also hold that sweetness for days after harvest.

GROWING
The best soil for sweet corn is sunny, well-drained, and loaded with nutrients. Corn is a hungry crop, and the soil should have at least three to four bushels of compost, or three to five pounds of a bagged organic fertilizer per 100 square feet. Corn should be sown one inch deep on the frost free date, but not before the soil has warmed to 65° F or so, spacing the

Corn Cultivars Sorted by Type		
Standard **(su)**	**Sugar** **(se/eh)**	**Supersweet** **(sh²)**
Earlivee Golden Cross Bantam Golden Jubilee Jubilee Seneca Chief Seneca Horizon Silver Queen	Alpine Platinum Lady Burgundy Delight Sugar Buns Clockwork Seneca Arrow Kandy Korn EH Starshine Kiss & Tell Tuxedo Miracle	Early Xtra-sweet Honey 'n Pearl How Sweet It Is Illini Xtra-sweet Northern Xtra-sweet Starstruck

seeds every two or three inches apart in the row.

We plant our sweet corn in a pair of rows, two feet apart, running the length of 30-inch-wide raised beds, and make sure that we plant two or three of these beds side by side. This way, we get four to six rows across. Because our beds are 24 feet long, this gives about 150 feet of corn in each planting. At one plant per foot final spacing, we average 200 ears or more per planting. A minimum planting would be about 50 to 60 plants, arranged in a square or round pattern for maximum wind pollination. For a succession harvest, either plant a number of varieties with a range of maturity dates, or plant your single favorite more than once, with the plantings a few weeks apart.

As soon as the sprouts are two or three inches high, we cultivate and thin them to about six inches apart. A few weeks later, once we are sure no further damage can come to the young seedlings, we remove every other plant, leaving one per foot. You should continue to cultivate until the plants are knee high; at that point they cast

'Seneca Horizon' sweet corn.

enough shade that most weeds won't be a problem.

Water is critical for corn throughout its life, but especially after the tassels have shed their pollen and the ears are beginning to swell. Three weeks after the silks appear, start checking the upper ears for ripeness. Peel back the tip of the husk and poke a tip kernel with your fingernail; it should shoot a milky sap. Closely note the state of the silks on the ripe ears, because, once you have learned to recognize the state of ripeness from the state of the silk, your harvest will proceed much more quickly.

HARVESTING
Don't harvest sweet corn until you are ready to cook it. Going out to the corn patch should be your last act before dinner, and the pot should be boiling with just an inch or two of water when you return and shuck out the ears. Take the tender inner husks and lay them in the bottom of the pot, directly in the water; then, lay the corn on top of the husks, just above the water. Let it steam for only one or two minutes; then remove it from the pot and take it right to the table.

POPCORN PRECAUTIONS
Popcorn and ornamental corn are grown by the same methods as sweet corn, but the ears are left on the plants until they are fully mature, dry, and the kernels hard. It is necessary to isolate popcorn from sweet corn, or the two may cross and ruin both. If you don't have the necessary hundred feet or so,

simply choose a late enough popcorn variety that won't start tasseling until your sweet corn has finished. Thus, they will thus be isolated in time, rather than in space.

CHOOSING THE BEST VARIETIES
The older, traditional kinds and early hybrid varieties are called *sugary* types. In catalogs or on seed packets you will see the code (**Su**) following the variety name; the first wave of new varieties are called *sugary enhanced* and are designated with the code (**Se**); the newest kinds are called *supersweet* and are coded (**Sh²**), a notation of their kernel type at planting time, which is shriveled, or shrunken (this is a material concern at planting and will be discussed again). Of these, we recommend planting primarily the sugary-enhanced (**Se**) types, as they have the best combination of flavor and ease of culture. The supersweets, unfortunately, need to be isolated a minimum of 100 feet (farther is better)

'Strawberry' popcorn.

from either field corn or other non-supersweet sweet corn varieties. If not, they will revert to their cattle corn ancestry, and it is a simple fact that even for the few gardeners who have that much room, supersweets are an unnecessary complication when the quality of the sugary enhanced varieties is so good.

Sweet corn is available with white kernels, with yellow kernels, and with a mixture of the two on the same ear. Of the standard, simple sugary (**Su**) types, the standard for white corn is 'Silver Queen', though it is not reliably early enough for the northern gardens (Zones 3 to 5). For those climates, the yellow hybrids 'Earlivee' and 'Seneca Horizon' are a better bet. Our choice for a standard bi-color is 'Burgundy Delight', which is not only reasonably early, but also has ornamental purple husks.

Among the sugary-enhanced (**Se**) kinds, we like 'Sugar Buns' and 'Seneca Arrow' for early yellows, 'Seneca Dawn' and 'Athos' for a bicolor, and 'Seneca Starshine' for a white. As noted earlier, we don't think that the supersweet (Sh^2) kinds are appropriate for home gardens.

Two caveats: sweet corn varieties change quickly, so any listing is, in essence, temporary, and sweet corn is very regional in its adaptation, so the best varieties may be specific to your region—ask your neighbors who have been gardening a while!

Our favorite popcorn variety is 'Strawberry', because the small ears, which resemble its namesake, are as ornamental as they are useful in the kitchen and make great arrangements.

Cucumbers

COMMON NAME
Cucumber

BOTANICAL NAME
Cucumis sativus

Nearly round 'Lemon' cucumbers.

RECOMMENDED ZONES (USDA)
ALL

Native to the East Indies and used by Asian cultures for millennia, the cucumber is no longer known in its wild form. By biblical times the cucumber reached Europe where it has become a staple, as it has in America.

Cucumbers are a fruiting vegetable adapted to training on trellises and fences. They are used raw in salads, pickled, or cooked. See the recipes for Cornichons, and Cucumber and Lemon Salad, on pages 129 and 130.

In smaller gardens, cucumber plants can be used as a visual barrier if grown on a trellis. It is too large a plant to grow on the ground in kitchen gardens.

The cucumber is a tropical plant, but one so fast-growing that there is nowhere in the lower 48 states where it can't be grown successfully. It is, however, very sensitive to even cool weather and dry conditions. It may not perform at its best in the far north or desert southwest without attention being paid to its needs. It is also, unfortunately, prone to foliage diseases in very humid climates.

GROWING
Cucumbers crave a rich soil, but don't get the soil out of whack by over-fertilizing. Too much nitrogen in relation to the other elements—especially phosphorus—will lead to large, leafy plants with few fruits; hardly what you want.

In all but the coldest, shortest seasons, cucumbers can be direct-sown. Wait until the ground is thoroughly warm and all danger of frost is past. You can place the seed one half to an inch deep in "hills"—groups of four to six seeds sown in a small raised mound, where compost has been mixed thoroughly with the soil. Each group is six feet (four feet for the new "bush" types) from its neighbors. Allow the plants to completely cover the area between—a method quite different from planting in rows. Or try what we do: sow four seeds to the foot down the middle of a standard three-foot-wide raised bed. We make these rows eight to 12 feet long, so that we can erect a trellis on which the cucumbers can climb.

Once the plants have emerged and spread their first few sets of true leaves (the serrated ones), thin the hills to the strongest three to four plants, or the rows to one plant per foot. Do this by cutting off the excess plants with a pair of scissors, not by pulling them out. That way you'll avoid disturbing adjacent plants and slowing their growth.

Cultivate the area between the hills or rows to prevent weeds. If you are growing on a trellis, erect it and lay the plants up against its base. A thick mulch of hay, straw or leaves

Cukes, ready for the pickling jars.

'Orient Express' cucumber.

will help retain soil moisture—and restrain weeds—through the season, and is an excellent idea for cucumbers.

HARVESTING

Cucumbers can be harvested any time after the fruits appear. Tiny ones for pickling have long been a French culinary specialty, but the best time is just after the small, spiny hairs on the surface of the fruit are no longer noticeable. Some types are hairless from the beginning. These are ready when they just start to look plump instead of wrinkled, and the skin picks up a shine. This may sound vague, but it is a very real difference and easily recognized with practice.

There is one yellow cucumber variety—called the 'Lemon cucumber' —with small, globe-shaped fruits, but for all other types, any color change toward yellow indicates that the fruits are past prime, and should be picked immediately, even if only for the chicken yard or compost pile. It is important to keep the fruits picked, even if you don't have an immediate use for them. Give them to a neighbor or the local food pantry; if allowed to ripen any fruits, the vines will stop producing.

PROTECTING

Trellising does wonders for combatting the foliage diseases that cucumbers are susceptible to, because it gets the

'Burpee Burpless' cucumbers.

plants up where air can circulate frequently around them. Immediately after planting, we put a floating row cover over the area so that the newly emerged seedlings won't be attacked by striped or spotted cucumber beetles. Right after sprouting is when they are most vulnerable.

CHOOSING THE BEST VARIETIES

There are a few different types of cucumbers. The standard dark green, smooth-skinned kinds, like 'Straight Eight' and the hybrid 'Sweet Success' are old standbys. There are also longer kinds, like those seen wrapped in plastic in the supermarkets. They are just as easy to grow; we like one called 'Orient Express', but there are many other good ones like 'Burpless' and 'Euro-American'.

Even better, though, is a hybrid called 'Amira' which is short and blocky, with a smooth, thin skin and fantastic yield.

For pickles, the 'Lemon' cucumber is excellent harvested small, as are the French cornichon types like 'Vert de Massy' and 'de Bourbonne'. The most unusual (also great for pickles) is the white (yes, pure white!) cucumber called 'de Bouneil', whose uncolored fruits allow the cook a little more creativity with pickle making!

SPECIAL NOTES

Cucumbers need water to grow well, and it is best supplied by drip irrigation so that the foliage stays dry. If you must water, do so before the late afternoon, so that there is time for

excess water to percolate or evaporate before evening. As long as the foliage dries off completely once every 18 hours, bacterial spores will not be able to establish themselves on the plants.

Long periods of rainy weather, when soil beneath unmulched plants splashes on to the leaves can be disastrous. If this happens, wait until the rain stops, then dust the leaves with powdered sulfur; this kills the spores before they have a chance to grow. It's really a better idea to use lots of mulch, instead.

---

e

Eggplant

COMMON NAMES
Eggplant

BOTANICAL NAME
Solanum melongena

RECOMMENDED ZONES (USDA)
4–10

Believed to have originated in southeast Asia from India to Thailand, eggplants were brought to Europe in the late Middle Ages, then to the Americas in the 17th century.

Cooks love the eggplant's adaptable nature in the kitchen or on the grill. Eggplants are native to southeast Asia, and difficult to grow in cool or cold climates. Eggplants themselves are quite beautiful and were first grown as ornamentals. The fruits come in a wide variety of colors, sizes and shapes.

'Violette de Firenze' eggplant.

'Easter Egg' eggplant.

They are used baked, sautéed, fried and grilled. See the recipe for Ratatouille on page 129.

GROWING

Eggplants require moderately rich soil and full sun in any climate. They are fruiting vegetables that take a moderate amount of space in the garden but are highly productive. Once out in the garden, they need 18 to 24 inches apiece to bear well.

Unless you have ample window sill space or a greenhouse, the best strategy for success is to buy nursery-grown plants. If you want to start your own (which is necessary if you want to grow some of the more interesting kinds), sow the seed in pots or flats, one-quarter inch deep, eight to 12 weeks before the last frost. They will not germinate well at less than 80° F. If you don't have a heat mat, consider putting the containers in the furnace room or on a warm shelf in the kitchen.

Once sprouted, the seedlings want as much light as they can get, and temperatures consistently above 65° F, even at night. Keep thinning the plants as they touch, doubling the space between

'Pintung Long' eggplant.

them with each thinning, so that they don't crowd and begin to stretch for the light. If each plant is in an individual pot, simply move the pots.

After all danger of frost and cool nights is over, and once the soil has warmed thoroughly, harden them off and set the plants out in the garden at the same level they were in the pots. Mulch, if possible.

HARVESTING

Eggplants are not usually harvested until at least one-third their mature size (check the catalog descriptions for this). Definitely, harvest before the fruits begin to lose their shine and get a golden undertone, at which time, seeds are forming and the texture will become dry.

PROTECTION

No more care will be necessary until harvest time unless the Colorado potato beetle finds them: eggplant is the only vegetable they prefer to potatoes. If they do appear, hand pick and crush the chunky black and orange striped adults. Then, inspect the plants for their bright orange eggs, which are laid on the underside of the leaves, and crush them, too. This "treasure hunt" is a great job for kids. If the eggs hatch, the larvae can be quite destructive. It may be necessary to

selectively dust infected plants with rotenone.

During hot, dry weather, flea beetles may be a problem. To protect the plants until they are large enough to resist, cover them with a floating row cover and don't remove it until they flower.

CHOOSING THE BEST VARIETIES

There are a wide variety of eggplants to grow in the kitchen garden from the small, bright fruits of 'Turkish Orange', which grows well only in hot summer areas, to miniature purples which are excellent for grilling, to larger white and purple kinds, and even some enormous, snake-like fruits in white, purple and green! Some suggestions: the antique Italian strains, 'Violetta di Firenze' and 'Violetta Lunga'; the whites, 'Easter Egg', 'Casper', or 'Osterei', or the Asian 'Pintung Long' and 'Thai Long Green'.

Flowers

The kitchen garden should definitely include flowers. Why? First, because some flowers are edible and make a final perfect addition to salads, especially; but also, as a garnish on soups, sandwiches, crudité-platters, or even desserts.

Cut flowers also fit into the kitchen garden because a table with flowers is a more inviting table. Dinner is improved by their presence, just as the garden itself benefits from their beauty.

Every kitchen garden needs flowers.

Cut flowers for the kitchen table.

Beyond flowers that you can eat, and those just for cutting, are fragrant flowers. In our own garden, we consider fragrant flowers an essential, because gardens, particularly kitchen gardens, are sensual gardens. We see the beauty of multi-colored lettuces, we hear the birds and the rustling of the corn, we taste the luscious sweetness of ripe melons and feel the rich soil as we search for our potato crop. Fragrant flowers add to this feast of the senses, making the garden a potent, magical experience.

Whether it's the lemony fragrance of 'Gem' marigolds as we brush by them at noon on our way to the salad patch, or the syrupy sweet, dusk-borne perfume of Nicotiana (flowering tobacco), the sense of smell definitely

White-flowered garlic chives.

Sunflowers—great for a vase!

completes the kitchen garden in a wonderful way.

GROWING

While there isn't room to discuss specific flowers in detail in this chapter, it is possible to summarize the types, their culture and their uses. All flowers fall into the same three categories of hardiness as vegetables, and, thus, the general guidelines for culture in Chapter 3 will work for them as well. One key thing to keep in mind, though: almost all flowers will grow well in the vegetable garden, but treat them as root crops in terms of fertility: too much nitrogen will produce large, leafy plants with fewer flowers.

The best way to handle cut flowers is to treat them just like vegetables: plant in beds for easy maintenance, harvest at their peak and replant regularly to have a constant supply. If space is limited, you may want your flowers to do double duty—both to grace the garden and for cutting. If you do, you'll just have to be more sparing with your cuts, so that the garden stays nice looking, too.

CHOOSING THE BEST VARIETIES

Though there are many edible flowers, we have had the best luck with nasturtiums, marigolds, calendulas, pansies and violas. The first two are

Calendulas, beautiful and edible.

tender annuals, while the next three are hardy. The flowers of many herbs and a good number of vegetables are also pretty enough to use as edible flowers. In all cases, the flower petals only are used if they will be mixed in with the dish, say a salad, while for garnish, the entire flower or even a sprig is more appropriate.

The choice of flowers for cutting is vast. If you are limited in space, favor packages of seed mixtures combined especially for cut flowers; if you have the room, or a preference for certain colors, you can be more selective. Our favorite flowers for cutting are zinnias, cosmos, sunflowers (make sure you choose types bred for smaller flowers, suitable for cutting), asters, pincushion flowers (*Scabiosa*), snapdragons and

'Jewel Mix' nasturtiums

bachelor's buttons (*Centaurea*). Don't forget to plant a few "fillers", like Baby's Breath (*Gypsophila*) to use in bouquets.

The key to fragrant flowers is to place them where they will have the most impact. Those that release their scent in the evening, like nicotiana and evening-scented-stocks, should be placed near areas where the family spends time after sunset or where the evening breeze will pick up the scent. We have an arbor where we picnic in the summer, surrounded by these and other fragrant plants like peonies, clethra, lilacs and angel's trumpet (*Brugmansia*), which should not be planted in gardens with small children around; it is poisonous. Plants like sweet alyssum and 'Gem' marigolds, both of which are dwarf plants and release their fragrance when brushed, make ideal edging plants for narrow walks.

Fruits

Even a small kitchen garden should include some fruit. These are usually divided into two types: small fruits, which include strawberries, raspberries (and other brambles), blueberries and grapes; and tree fruits, such as apples, pears, peaches, plums, apricots and cherries.

SMALL FRUITS
Strawberries
Small fruits have the benefit of bearing younger than tree fruits—some as soon as two months after planting—and requiring less care and equipment.

Although strawberries take some management, the rewards are definitely worth it.

The simplest and most space-efficient of the small fruits is the strawberry. There are two types: alpine strawberries, which bear tiny, flavor-packed fruits and grow as compact clumps (excellent for edging), and regular strawberries, which have larger fruits and put out runners which will root themselves in nearby soil to make new "daughter" plants. Either can be grown in pots, though the Alpine kinds like 'Baron Solemacher' or the new pink flowered 'Pink Panda™' are tidier. Grow regular strawberries in hanging baskets so that the runners can cascade over the side.

In the garden, strawberries prefer a rich, well-drained soil in full sun. Most gardeners plant strawberries from purchased plants (make sure they are certified virus-free) in the spring for harvest the following two to three years (after the second season, the daughter plants can be cut loose

from their parents and used to start a new planting).

GROWING
There are a number of planting systems for growing strawberries. We prefer a simple, one-foot spacing in beds with all the runners removed from the plants, unless it is time to establish another bed. The most important thing to remember is that the plants should be set in the bed so that the crown—the spot where the roots and tops meet—is exactly at ground level; otherwise the plants will not perform well. Mulch the plants well with straw to preserve moisture and remove any flowers that form the first season.

CHOOSING THE BEST VARIETIES
Some of the best flavored "spring bearing" strawberries are 'Catskill', 'Honeoye', and 'Sparkle' (which has the benefit of being a late bloomer and one of the most likely varieties to miss the late spring frosts that sometimes ruin the harvest of earlier kinds). Our favorite, however, is the "day-neutral" variety 'Tri-star', which not only bears throughout the summer and until the first hard frost, but also can be picked the first spring as well—only two months after planting! With the runners removed, it makes an excellent edging plant as well.

Bramble Fruits
Bramble fruits, like raspberries, blackberries, and loganberries, are easy to grow if you have the room and keep plants under control. They will

'Honeoye' strawberries.

'Pink Panda' strawberry blossoms.

Small, flavorful 'Alpine' strawberries.

'Fall Gold' raspberries.

'Cumberland' black raspberries.

'Thornfree' blackberries.

A bumper crop of raspberries.

Loganberries.

Luscious gooseberries.

continue to provide a harvest for 15 to 20 years if well maintained. Because they grow four to six feet tall, berry plants make excellent divider plants, visually indicating the boundary between two parts of the garden.

GROWING
Purchase raspberry plants certified to be virus-free. They will thrive in any well-drained vegetable garden soil with normal yearly fertilization. Space plants every two to three feet along a three- to four-foot-wide bed, and plant so the crown is just at soil level. Mulch the soil around the plants heavily with straw, hay or bark, both to preserve moisture and keep the soil cool, and to retard weeds, which can be a real nuisance in a berry patch.

CHOOSING THE BEST VARIETIES
Our favorite summer-bearing varieties are 'Viking', which is super vigorous, 'Canby' and 'Taylor' for their exceptional fruit, and 'Titan' for its exceptional vigor and earliness. Of the fall bearers, our favorites are 'Fall Gold' (yes, the berries are gold), 'Fall Red' and 'Heritage'.

Blueberries
Blueberries are shrubs, but unlike many of the other beautiful shrubs in the home landscape, they also bear a large crop of delicious fruits for many, many years. Unfortunately they are not well acclimated to large parts of the U.S. They only grow well in highly acid soils (which excludes much of the west), and where the summers don't

get too hot (except for the so-called "rabbiteye blueberries" which will do well in the south).

GROWING
If you are in an appropriate area, buy plants in early spring, and set them out four to six feet apart in a moist, acid soil in full sun or very light shade, at the same depth they were in the pot. Mulch well with an acid mulch like bark or pine needles.

After the plants are established for a year or two, you can affect the quality and quantity of the crop by a program of judicious pruning. Blueberries bear best on two-year-old branches, so the basic management principle is to remove the oldest third of the bush every year in late winter, basically

A bumper blueberry harvest.

Currants, ready for jam.

cutting out the oldest branches so the bush is composed of only one- and two-year-old wood. By doing so, you'll have young vigorous branches coming into production every year.

CHOOSING THE BEST VARIETIES

Because blueberries do not self-pollinate readily, buy at least three bushes, mixing the kinds. Some good choices are 'Earliblue', 'Blueray', 'Bluecrop', 'Patriot' and 'Northblue'. In the south, the favorite rabbiteye variety is 'Tifblue'.

Two other bush fruits you might like to try, if you have the space, are gooseberries and currants. Be sure to check with your local extension office first, though, as there is a prohibition on growing these fruits in some parts of the country because they are an alternate host for diseases of agriculturally important crops.

TREE FRUITS

While the subject of growing fruit trees could—and does—occupy a whole shelf of books, we should address it here because of the ways fruit trees fit into the overall design and enjoyment of kitchen gardens.

In general terms, fruit trees which reach six to eight feet tall are called dwarf; semi-dwarf varieties reach 10 to 16 feet tall; while standard fruit trees will usually reach 20 to 36 feet tall, and as wide across, depending on the

Pears, long-lived and bountiful.

Home garden treat: fresh apricots.

species. Choose the type of fruit tree carefully, taking into account the scale of the rest of the garden, remembering that only the largest gardens wouldn't be over-shadowed (literally) by a standard-sized tree.

When choosing the kind of tree fruit to grow, keep in mind that peaches and sweet cherries do best in USDA Zones 5–8, while sour cherries and plums can survive Zone 4 winter temperatures. Most apples do best in Zones 4–7, as do pears, though in all these cases, specific varieties may stretch the range both north and south. Late season frosts are always threats to blossoms and affect the entire harvest. The best way to find

Space-saving apple training.

Plums, for fresh use or jams.

'Jonagold' apples.

out which varieties are well-suited to your area is to ask other fruit growers and check with your county extension agent.

Many varieties of tree fruit require pollination by another variety of the same species, and, thus, you will need at least two trees, even if only one is inside the bounds of your kitchen garden. Inquire before you buy the trees. This information is on the variety tag. A knowledgeable salesperson should know what pollinates what. Again, your extension agent can help you here.

....
g

Garlic

COMMON NAMES
Garlic

BOTANICAL NAME
Allium sativum

RECOMMENDED ZONES (USDA)
ALL

What kitchen garden could be thought complete without garlic? High-yielding (on a square foot basis), relatively trouble free and easy to grow if you follow a few simple rules, the "stinking rose" is a must-grow crop.

One of the most venerated and ancient plants in the kitchen garden, garlic was widely used by the ancient Chinese, Egyptians, Greeks and Romans. It is no less revered by the modern cook. Garlic is an antioxidant and contains the trace element selenium. It is used in seasoning, baking and grilling.

GROWING

Use bulblets; in the kitchen garden, garlic is not grown from seed. The trick to good garlic is to understand that, even in the far north, it is a fall-planted, next-summer-harvested crop. Take a clove of garlic (best from a farmer's market), break it into individual cloves and stick them, eight inches apart each way, into deeply prepared soil, root end down, until the pointed upward tip is half an inch beneath the surface. You can tell the root end by the raised ridge around the edge, that represents the junction between where the roots will grow and where the tops will grow.

Garlic plants, about to flower.

Young garlic plants.

Planting time is the same as for daffodils or tulips: early enough in the fall, so that the bulb can begin to grow, but late enough so that the growing tip of the plant will not break out of the soil and be damaged by sub-zero temperatures. In mild climates, the plants will grow all winter; in cold climates, they will wait until spring.

The second key to good garlic—in fact all members of the onion family—is to remember that while we think of them as root crops, they are actually leaf crops and need a relatively high nitrogen level when they are young. The way we provide this is to give them a shot of liquid fish fertilizer in mid-spring, shortly after they have started to grow. This gives them an immediate boost, but is gone by the time they are ready to harden off their bulbs—a time when nitrogen is to be avoided, or the bulbs will be soft and keep poorly.

After harvesting, garlic should be air-cured for at least a week.

HARVESTING

Keep the plants well weeded until mid-summer, when the tops will wither and die down. Then, at the beginning of a two to three day dry spell, lift the bulbs and allow them to sit on the surface of the soil before moving them to a dark, dry place to cure atop screens for another week. Once cured, the tops can be braided together or simply cut off, and the bulbs stored in mesh bags in a dry location that is 50 to 70° F and relatively low humidity—below 50 percent, at least.

PROTECTING

Root and crown rot problems are best avoided by rotating garlic, instead of growing it in the same bed year after year.

CHOOSING THE BEST VARIETIES

'Italian Purple Skin'; 'California Late'; 'New York White'.

....

h

....

Herbs

A kitchen garden without herbs hardly deserves the name. You can grow a large variety of herbs in any size garden. A patio container garden has room for basil, thyme and others. Or if you do have plenty of room, but your climate is harsh, you might want to

The many colors and forms of basil.

Experienced gardeners know to contain invasive mints in a pot.

bring a few plants inside for the winter, neatly potted up in late summer for fresh harvest through the winter.

In general herbs are grown just like vegetables, except they are less fussy about soil. Almost all kinds are available as young plants from your local garden center, but many gardeners prefer to start from seed. Be sure to weed thoroughly—mulching is always a good idea—and water regularly.

The up-and-coming herb in kitchen gardens today is **Basil** (*Ocimum basilicum*), a tender annual. Treat the seed and seedlings just as you would eggplant, and you won't go wrong. Garden spacing is eight inches apart for the dwarf kinds like 'Basilico

Greco', 'Spicy Globe' and 'Piccolo Verde Fino' (Fine Green)—all great for salads. Give a foot apiece to the standard pesto basil, 'Sweet Genovese', its variants, and the 'Cinnamon', 'Licorice', and 'Lemon' basils, as well as the purple leaved 'Opal' and 'Red Rubin' basils, that make such choice and unique vinegars. Large kinds, like the lettuce-leaved 'Napoletano' and 'Mammoth', should have 18 inches to develop the huge leaves that are their trademark. Once you have had pesto-basted scrod, wrapped in 'Mammoth' basil leaves and then grilled, you won't begrudge them the extra room!

Basil, like virtually all herbs, should be harvested just as the flowers are about to open; after that time the

The uniform 'Spicy Globe' basil.

Flat-leaved Italian parsley.

Dill weed, in full flower.

Greek oregano flowers.

Summer savory.

Bronze and green fennel.

intensity of the flavor decreases. Harvest in early morning for best texture, or in late afternoon for maximum flavor.

The most common garden herb is the biennial **Parsley** (*Petroselinum crispum*), often grown as an annual. If you don't purchase plants, start the seed indoors eight to 12 weeks before the last frost, and set out in the garden a foot apart after the last hard frost, six to eight weeks later. If you direct-sow a

second planting at that time, you can have young, fresh leaves to pick not only through the summer and fall, but the direct-sown plants will overwinter and provide a spring harvest before running to seed, just about the time

the next spring's indoor-sown plants begin to yield—nearly a year-round harvest!

After extensive taste tests, our favorite curly-leaf parsley is the Dutch variety 'Krausa'. Flat-leaved Italian parsley is almost always more strongly flavored than the curly kinds, but not as ornamental on the plate.

Dill (*Anethum graveolens*) is simplicity itself to grow. Direct seed in a sunny, well-drained spot after the

Cilantro and Chinese cabbage.

Chive flowers.

Tarragon, with sage in front.

danger of hard frost is past, setting the seed about one-half inch deep, 12 seeds to the foot, in rows eight inches apart. When the seedlings are four to six inches tall, thin them to six inches apart, gradually, using the thinnings in your mesclun salad mix. Plant more every two weeks or so until about 60 days before hard frost. If you want dill flower heads, let one of the plantings grow to full size; even before then the foliage is useful for seasoning. Our favorite variety is 'Dukat', also known as Tetra Dill, a compact, but high-yielding strain.

Both green and bronze **Fennel** (*Foeniculum vulgare*) are grown just like dill for salads and seasoning, but allow at least a foot per plant. If you plant the kind known as bulbing or Florence fennel, the base of the plant will swell into large bulbs that are a specialty of Italian cuisine (see the recipe for Fried Fennel on page 131). For this, use the Swiss variety 'Zefa Fino'.

The green salad and seasoning fennel will not bulb up; neither will the bronze fennel, though the variety 'Smokey' will make extremely attractive flower heads that are great in dried flower arrangements if thinned to eight to 12 inches apart.

Another herb that has seen a huge increase in popularity over the last ten years or so is **Cilantro** (*Coriandrum sativum*), the leaves of the coriander plant. Special strains, like 'Slobolt', have been developed that extend the period of leaf harvest far beyond what used to be possible. Sow the seed directly in the garden every two weeks from mid-spring to late summer, 12 seeds to the inch, one-half inch deep; thin the plants gradually for table use until they stand eight to 12 inches apart. Once the broad leaves give way to thin, bristly leaves, either pull up the plants or just allow them to set seed and harvest it for your own coriander.

There are two forms of **Savory**, winter and summer, members of two closely related species (*Satureja horten-*

The various types of sage are as ornamental as they are flavorful.

sis and *S. montana*). For the kitchen garden we recommend staying with summer savory, which is easy to start from seed eight to 12 weeks before the last frost and set out in the garden six to eight weeks later. Give the plants a foot apiece and they will grow into small, woody, shrub-like plants with small, dark green leaves and beautiful lavender flowers. What you don't use in the kitchen can be bunched and dried for herbal wreaths.

Aside from its many uses in the kitchen, perennial **Thyme** (*Thymus vulgaris*) makes an excellent edging plant for herb beds or kitchen gardens in general, because of its compact growth habit, only eight to 12 inches tall, absolute winter hardiness and a variety of scents, flavors and flower colors. Try lemon thyme, caraway thyme, or gold- and silver-edged thyme. Keep in mind that some of these special types do not come true from seed, and must be propagated by cuttings or division. Our favorite culinary thyme is called 'French' summer thyme, which has larger leaves than the 'German' winter thyme.

Oregano (*Origanum vulgare*) comes

Harvesting young parsley.

in both culinary and ornamental forms and is a hardy perennial. The white-flowered forms, while perhaps not as aesthetic, are more flavorful. We prefer so-called Greek oregano (*O. heraclitum*), which doesn't make much of an edging, but does make a great pasta sauce or pizza topping.

Sage (*Salvia officinalis*) has relatively large seeds and is very easy to grow. Start it at about the same time as the thyme, sowing the seed one-half inch deep and setting the plants out in the garden one foot apart each way, after the last hard frost. As with the perennials above, there are ornamental forms, but in the case of sage, most are considerably less hardy, so in Zone 4 and colder you may need to pot them up and take them inside for the winter. The time to transplant them is about a month before the end of good outside growing weather; that way they will have a chance to adjust to their new quarters.

Chives and their close relatives, **garlic chives** (*Allium schoenoprasum* and *A. tuberosum*, respectively) should be started indoors just as if they were leeks, using the same schedule and planting instructions. As both make excellent edging plants, be sure to plant plenty, although garlic chives can sometimes become invasive. Chives have pink blossoms in a globe and tubular, hollow leaves that taste like a mild scallion. Garlic chives' flowers are white, grow in a more open habit and sit atop flat, strap-like leaves with a mellow garlic flavor. Both are incredibly hardy, long-lived perennials about 18 to 24 inches tall, and are easy

to divide in the spring to make more plants. Both are real kitchen garden workhorses.

The true **French tarragon** (*Artemisia dracunculus*), so beloved of cooks, does not come true from seed, so buy your first plants from a nursery. Be sure to smell and taste the exact plant you intend to buy, since all of the cuttings and divisions you may make from it in future years will be absolute copies of the mother plant. There is some variation in the plants available in the trade. Even better, get some from a friend. Above all, don't bother with tarragon seed, which is Russian tarragon, a different and inferior plant.

Tarragon likes a dry, somewhat infertile soil and may die out if planted in a moist, rich soil, especially at the northern edge of its hardiness range—borderline Zone 3–4.

k

Kale & Collards

COMMON NAMES
Kale; Collard Greens

BOTANICAL NAME
Brassica napus; Brassica oleracea

RECOMMENDED ZONES (USDA)
ALL

Kale and collards are essentially non-heading cabbages, and are among the oldest forms of cultivated plants in the brassica family. They are often quite ornamental and always nutritious.

Kale is the most basic of the *Brassicas* (cabbage family), and certainly, along with collards, the easiest to grow. For our purposes, they are treated the same, though kale is more widely grown in the north, and collards in the south. Collards tolerate heat better than any other cabbage-family member.

'Peacock' ornamental kale.

GROWING
Both can be grown as a spring crop, sown direct in the garden as soon as the ground can be worked in spring, but the best-tasting crops are harvested in the fall. To facilitate handling, we start with seedlings.

Sow the seed in flats or pots about 90 days before the onset of cool fall weather. Thin the plants as they touch, until at about four weeks of age, they have a minimum of two inches apiece. Set out in a well-prepared, rich soil with full sun, 18 to 24 inches apart each way. Then simply keep the rows or beds weeded until frost.

Kale with flowering red salvia.

Even edible kales are good looking.

HARVESTING

Once there have been two or three solid frosts, harvest by removing the largest individual leaves from the plants and leaving the small leaves at the center of the plant to grow. They will provide a continuous harvest throughout the winter, unless killed by cold, and can survive temperatures well down into the teens.

PROTECTING

Kale and collards are technically susceptible to all the pests of the cabbage family, but in practice, are little bothered by either root maggots or leaf eaters.

Highly ornamental pink kale.

CHOOSING THE BEST VARIETIES

Look for such names as 'Siberian', 'Vates', or the hybrid 'Winterbor'. There are also ornamental varieties which, while not as tasty as those just mentioned, make an incredible display planting, while still providing colorful leaves for garnishes.

Kohlrabi

COMMON NAMES
Kohlrabi, Sputnik

BOTANICAL NAME
Brassica oleracea

RECOMMENDED ZONES (USDA)
ALL

Kohlrabi has been grown in Central Europe for centuries. It is increasing in popularity in America.

One of the least known, yet one of the most useful members of the cabbage family, Kohlrabi is a quick growing crop that provides enormous amount of good eating in a small space. Peel and slice kohlrabi for a crudite platter, or grate and sauté as you would potato pancakes. See the recipe for Grated Kohlrabi on page 135.

GROWING

Hot climate gardeners may want to limit themselves to spring and fall crops, as most cabbage family plants don't taste as good if matured during hot weather.

Here in the north, we plant continuous crops every two to three weeks from early spring up until 60 days before hard frost. Direct-sow one quarter inch deep in rows eight to 12 inches apart, thinned to six inches apart after the first true leaves appear. The bulbs, which are actually swollen stems, will be ready in 45 to 60 days.

HARVESTING

Harvest any time after the bulbous stem reaches an inch in diameter.

'Early Purple Vienna' kohlrabi.

The leafy, cool-loving kohlrabi.

'Early White Vienna' kohlrabi.

PROTECTING

The leaves are sometimes bothered by cabbage worms and loopers, but unless totally defoliated, the plants will continue to produce bulbs. As a result, the pests are of little concern. Standard controls will work, however, if necessary (see broccoli).

CHOOSING THE BEST VARIETIES

There are a number of beautiful hybrid kohlrabi, but we have found that the best tasting are the old-fashioned varieties, 'White Vienna' and 'Purple Vienna'; for a real whopper, try the variety 'Gigant', which is the favorite of central European gardeners. Given 18 to 24 inches apiece these monsters can reach up to a foot across, and weigh as much as 20 to 30 pounds, yet still stay tender and flavorful!

Leeks

COMMON NAMES
Leek, Flag

BOTANICAL NAME
Allium porrum / Allium ampeloprasum

RECOMMENDED ZONES (USDA)
ALL

Native to Mediterranean soils, leeks have a very long cultural history and are highly prized in many countries. The Welsh, for example, revere them. Most Americans have eaten only store-bought leeks, which aren't as good as what you can grow. See the recipes for Leek and Sausage Pie, and for Potato and Leek Soup, on pages 134 and 137.

GROWING
Despite their appearance as a long-shanked member of the onion family, leeks are a leaf crop and like a rich, well-drained, looser soil.

Fresh harvest of winter leeks.

A large number of leeks can be grown in a small space if you place them 6 inches apart in all directions in a well-prepared bed with good loose soil. Their sole handicap is that they require a long season. It was once thought that they required special attention as well, but there are some

Sculptural beauty of leeks.

simple tricks to get around this. Remember that this is a leaf crop, so the soil should be deeply worked, rich in nutrients and able to drain well, so that you can provide ample water without soaking the soil.

Sow seed in flats or pots a full 12 weeks before the last hard frost for your area, and as soon as the little "flag leaf" characteristic of the onion family unfolds. Use a pair of fine point scissors to snip off all but one plant per half inch. This will get them off to a quick start and provide large, but tender leeks in the end. They do not need very warm temperatures, but should have full sun until the danger of hard frost is past, at which time they can be hardened off and then set out in the garden four to eight inches apart (use the closer spacing if you'd like to harvest every other one for "baby leeks" in mid-summer). Ideally, they will be six to eight inches tall at this point, with a stem about the diameter of a knitting needle.

The work in leeks used to be in blanching them. This was done either by trenching or by banking up soil or mulching around the stems in early fall. If you properly prepare the soil before planting, there are easier ways. One is to take the handle of an upside down hoe and use it to poke holes six to eight inches deep where each plant will go; then simply place the seedlings, one to a hole, so the youngest leaf just protrudes above the soil surface. If rain is not imminent, turn on the sprinkler. This will settle the soil in the hole around the roots at the bottom and provide automatic blanching for the lower part of the stem.

HARVESTING
Leeks can be harvested at any time, but because they are so hardy, are usually left in place until late fall. Then they are dug as needed and used as a flavoring for soups. Tender specimens make an excellent stand-alone vegetable, sliced lengthwise and sautéed with a bit of butter.

'Blue Solaise', 'King Richard', 'Nebraska'.

Lettuce

COMMON NAMES
Lettuce

BOTANICAL NAME
Lactuca sativa

RECOMMENDED ZONES (USDA)
ALL

Native to the Near East and the Mediterranean, lettuce is (and should be) one of the top crops in a kitchen garden. It is easy to grow and very productive, and it's one of those crops where the quality difference between store-bought and home-grown is greatest.

GROWING AND CHOOSING THE BEST VARIETIES

Lettuce wants a rich, well-drained soil. In the north, it is grown in full sun, except during the middle of the summer, but in the south or the arid west, it is a good candidate for partly shady areas where other vegetable crops might suffer. With a little attention, it can be grown nearly year round in all but the hottest and coldest parts of the country.

Lettuce is classified into four groups based on plant habit: loose-leaf, butterhead, crisphead and romaine.

Loose-leaf lettuces are ideal for cutting, but will form large open heads if given the room. They are, in general,

A variety of lettuces creates a tapestry-like effect.

'Buttercrunch' lettuce.

'LolloBionda' and 'Lollo Rosso'.

'Summertime' lettuce.

the earliest. Some good varieties to try are 'Red (and Green) Salad Bowl', 'Royal Oak Leaf', 'Grand Rapids' and various forms of 'Simpson'. One special class of tiny, Italian, loose-leaf lettuces, called 'Lollo Bionda', and 'Lollo Rosso', are often used for edging ornamental kitchen gardens, because of the uniform habit, strong color and heat tolerance.

Butterhead lettuces are the soft, tender heading lettuces seen in the market: all the way from the tiny "Bibb" and its variants to the larger, so-called "Boston" types, and a range of fine European varieties like 'Esmeralda' and 'Ostinata' in green, or the French 'Merveille des Quatres Saisons' (Four Seasons) or 'Sierra' in red. The more substantial 'Buttercrunch' and 'Matchless' types are considered part of the Butterhead clan.

Crisphead lettuces include the iceberg types, like 'Crispino', 'Great Lakes' and 'Summertime'. And they,

Harvesting lettuce at the peak of tender perfection.

too, include some red forms, like 'Rosa' and 'Cerise'.

Romaine lettuces are the upright, thick-leaved lettuces used for Caesar salads, and they, too, come in both green and red. Our favorites for the green include: 'Apollo', which is especially adapted to early spring crops under covers: 'Ballon', which is especially heat tolerant, and the reds, 'Rouge d'Hiver' and 'Rosalita'. As with

loose-leaf, there is a miniature type known as 'Little Gem', or 'Diamond Gem' that produces tight, tiny heads that are ideal for making a "hearts of Romaine" salad.

There are two basic ways to grow lettuce: for heads, or for cutting. Our discussion will be broken down along these lines. When we grow lettuce for heads, whether the tight, iceberg types, or the tender and frilly loose-leaf types, we start the seed in flats or pots so that we can more precisely control the timing and spacing of the crop.

Sow the seed only a quarter-inch deep, water from below, and when the seedlings show their first true leaves, thin by cutting off the overcrowded plants. Lettuce will germinate in as little as 72 hours at temperatures between 65 and 75° F, but most varieties will go dormant if the soil temperature is above 80° F. Thus our spring and fall crops germinate without much attention, while summer crops should be started

'Royal Oakleaf' lettuce.

'Ballon' lettuce.

A raised bed planting of lettuce.

in a cool spot, like a basement or cool garage. In any case, the seedlings should have bright light as soon as they sprout to keep them stocky.

After the danger of really hard frost in spring, set the plants out eight to 12 inches apart each way (some varieties, such as the loose-leaf types 'Salad Bowl' and 'Red Sails' will grow very large if allowed more room). During hot, dry periods, wait until evening or the beginning of a cloudy period to transplant. Make sure that they get watered within a few hours after setting out. Keep them cultivated and well watered until they fill in the intervening bed space, then harvest.

For the most tender, longest-lasting harvest, we grow lettuce for cutting. To do this, direct-sow a quarter inch deep in rows only six to eight inches apart, anytime the soil can be worked. If the air or soil temperature is above 80° F, water immediately after sowing with cold water, then lay a two by eight foot board of appropriate length over the top of the row. This insulates the row from the heat of the sun and allows the lettuce to germinate. Check the row each morning and remove the board as soon as there is any evidence of sprouting. If you sowed the seed sparsely—only two or three seeds to the inch—no thinning will be necessary.

Here in the north, we put a floating row cover over the very first planting to temper the temperature swings of early spring; later on, when the weather is consistently hot, we rig up a piece of shade cloth to help cool the bed. Screens work just as well and can be easily propped up off the ground on concrete blocks. When cold weather arrives in the fall, we switch back to row covers, and in winter, to a few short rows in the cold frame. Using this method, we can have fresh salads from April until December. Harvest by cutting the plants off an inch above the ground, when they are only four to six inches tall; then water, and they will grow again. A few short rows sown every two to three weeks will provide a constant supply of young lettuces for the salad bowl, only four to six weeks after sowing.

HARVESTING

Harvest lettuce heads by cutting just above the ground with scissors or a sharp knife about 60 to 80 days after transplant, depending on the type.

PROTECTING

One of the major pests of lettuce is aphids. If necessary, they can be controlled with special horticultural soap sprays, available at garden centers or by mail. As with all pest controls, follow the label instructions carefully. These sprays are also effective for whiteflies, which can be a problem in warm, wet seasons or climates.

Melons

COMMON NAMES
Cantaloupe, Muskmelon, Melon

BOTANICAL NAME
Cucumis melo

RECOMMENDED ZONES (USDA)
ALL

Melons are a garden delicacy. A well-grown cantaloupe, casaba, or charentais is a wonder and a pleasure that no one but a gardener will ever know in its fullest.

Melons can be grown just like cucumbers, but because they are so much more flavorful, more attention should be paid to watering and pruning of the plants. Why? Because melons are watery plants by nature, like cucumbers, and for them to have their best flavor, you want to balance the water needs of the growing plant with the water needs of the fruit-maturing plant.

'Charantais' melon.

'Piel de Sapor' cantaloupe.

Hybrid 'Charantais' melon.

'Galia' melon.

GROWING

For the kitchen garden, melons should be given their own bed or, for smaller types, raised on a moderate trellis, like cucumbers. Give your melons a rich soil and full sun, but as with other fruiting plants, make sure that the nutrients are properly balanced. Too much nitrogen in relation to phosphorus will lead to huge green plants with few fruits and little flavor.

We start out melons in small pots, two weeks before the last spring frost. Plant two or three seeds half an inch deep in three to four inch pots. Once they have their first true leaves, remove all but the strongest. Germination temperature should be 80° F or more. During the growth of the seedlings, they should not be allowed to cool below 65° F, suffer for water or become crowded. Once frost is past and the weather has become settled, the hardened-off plants should be planted promptly. Choose an overcast day. Set a foot apart in rows six feet apart, then water if rain is not imminent.

Keep melon plants well watered when they are young, but once the melons reach four inches or so in diameter, stop watering. This causes the flavor constituents of the fruits to concentrate and will make for better-tasting melons. A mulch of hay, straw or leaves will help to keep soil moisture levels adequate without diluting the flavor of the harvest.

American muskmelons are ready to harvest when the fruits separate from the vine with just a light tug; European and some Asian types must be cut from the vine. In either case, though, ripeness can be recognized both by the shading of the background skin color toward yellow gold, as well as by a ripe fragrance at the blossom end (the end not connected to the stem), which also will become soft to the touch at maturity.

CHOOSING THE BEST VARIETIES

The types of melons are nearly endless. Among standard cantaloupes, some of the best are 'Ambrosia', 'Athena' and the super early 'Earlisweet'. Green-fleshed types that will reward the kitchen gardener include 'Galia' and 'Passport'. There are many other kinds, as well: 'Santa Claus' or 'Christmas' melons, 'Casabas', Italian 'Piel de Sapor', and perhaps best known of the specialty melons, the 'Charantais', including 'Savor' and 'Alienor'.

PROTECTING

If cucumber beetles are a problem in your area, as they are in ours, cover the plants with a floating row cover, immediately after planting; this will also protect them from any last minute cool spells.

O

Okra

COMMON NAMES
Okra, Gumbo Plant

BOTANICAL NAME
Abelmoschus esculentus

RECOMMENDED ZONES (USDA)
4–10

Okra originates from Africa and is actually a form of hibiscus, and a very ornamental vegetable with large hollyhock-like flowers. It can be grown as a specimen plant. Okra is used in soups, stews or stir-fries and is a staple of southern cooking.

Once relegated exclusively to southern gardens and southern kitchens, okra has now gone nationwide. Smaller, faster-growing, more cold-tolerant varieties like 'Annie Oakley' and 'Blondy' can be grown just about anywhere in the continental United States.

GROWING

Okra needs a rich soil, not too high in nitrogen, full sun and good drainage.

Gardeners in short season areas should start the plants inside a month before last frost. Set out in the garden 12 to 18 inches apart after all danger of frost is past and the soil is thoroughly warm.

HARVESTING

Harvest the young seed pods when they are only three to four inches long, every other day or so, to prevent the plant from actually ripening any seed,

'Red River' okra.

Okra's hisbiscus-like flowers.

or it will stop producing. Try not to bruise them while picking, as this makes them slimy during cooking.

CHOOSING THE BEST VARIETIES

Old fashioned kinds grow up to seven feet tall. After years of intensive breeding, newer varieties grow only three to four feet tall, which is much more manageable for the kitchen garden.

Other varieties beyond the two mentioned earlier are 'Burgundy', an All America Award winner that bears colorful red pods in only 60 days on four-foot plants, and the traditional variety 'Clemson Spineless', up to five feet tall and a very high yielder.

Onions

COMMON NAMES
Onion

BOTANICAL NAME
Allium cepa

RECOMMENDED ZONES (USDA)
ALL

Natives of Asia and now used worldwide, onions are one of the oldest cultivated crops. Despite their availability in the market year round, they are an excellent candidate for the kitchen garden. The reason is simple: most of the onions you buy in the market, and all of the onion sets that you can buy at garden centers in the springtime are pungent, long-keeping varieties. Yet for the kitchen gardener who will grow them from seed, there are many, many more kinds of onions available.

Onions are used as seasoning in soups and stews, grilled, fried, and sautéed; some forms are used fresh in salads and on sandwiches. See the recipes for Ratatouille, and for Fresh Hot Salsa, on pages 132.

GROWING

Despite its use in a bulb form, the onion is a leaf crop and wants rich, moist soil. There are two factors that matter when choosing what kind of onions to grow: your latitude and whether you plan to store your onions for off-season use. Storage onions are

Set for the winter: a golden harvest of braided onions.

'Walla Walla Sweet' onions.

Laying the harvest out to dry.

'Italian Red Torpedo' onions.

pungent, and for good reason: it is the sulfur compounds in the onion that kill any bacteria that would lead to rot in storage. So called "sweet onions", which will not keep more than a couple of months in storage, actually do not have any higher sugar levels than more pungent and better storing onions, only lower sulfur levels. The reason onions from Vidalia, Georgia and Walla Walla, Washington are so mild is that growers there use low sulfur varieties grown in low sulfur soils, thus yielding especially mild, sweet onions!

Latitude matters because most onions are sensitive to day length and this varies by latitude. South of the 35th parallel, the days never get really long, while up along the Canadian border, summer days can reach almost 15 hours in length.

Thus, in the south, gardeners plant what are called "short-day" (SD) onions in the fall, then harvest a month or two after the spring equinox (when the day length is 12 hours), which triggers the bulbing reflex. In the north, "long-day" (LD) onions are

started indoors, then set out in mid-spring and harvested a month or two after the summer solstice, which triggers their bulbing reflex.

Onions need a rich, well-drained soil to produce large bulbs, which are actually layer upon layer of swollen leaf bases. During the early part of their growth, they need plentiful nitrogen, but once bulbing starts, too much nitrogen leads to double bulbs and poor storage. The same is true for water: lots early on, but very little when the bulbs are forming is best. It is critically important to control weeds, because onions do not compete well with broad-leaved plants. If you use a mulch, pull it back

'Granex' onions.

away from the bulbs once they begin to swell.

In the south, sow a short-day variety in August or September, a quarter to a half inch deep in rows eight to 12 inches apart. Once the single seed (or "flag") leaf unfolds, thin the plants to an inch apart. Over the course of the fall and winter, continue thinning by harvesting alternate plants for green onions, until the remaining plants are three to four inches apart.

In the north you can follow a similar schedule, but with long-day onions, as long as your minimum winter temperature doesn't get much below 0° F without snow cover. This is how Walla Walla onions are grown. We start seed in trays at the end of February (a full 12 weeks before the last frost) and grow them exactly as we do leeks. Once the danger of hard frost is past, we set the onion seedlings out four to eight inches apart, depending on how large an onion we want. Any extras get set in left over spaces to be pulled for green onions. At the same time, we seed a row or two of a non-bulbing type to use once these leftovers are gone. Harvest for long-day onions is the same as for short-day, but will occur in late July or August according to the maturity rate of the variety. Northern gardeners can also grow small pickling or boiling onions by planting short-day types as soon as the ground can be worked in spring; they will bulb early and small.

HARVESTING
In early summer, after half the tops have died down, pull the plants at the beginning of a dry spell. Allow them to cure on the surface of the soil for two or three days, then move them to a dimly lit dry area where they can continue to dry off the ground. (We use screens propped up on cement blocks in the carport.) Once dry, the tops can be braided or removed and the onions stored in mesh bags. The longest storage life is at 50 to 60° F and 25 to 45 percent humidity.

CHOOSING THE BEST VARIETIES
Recommended Short-Day Onions
There are few long-keeping storage types for southern gardeners, but sweet onions galore. Try Bermuda types, one of the Texas 'Grano' family or the hybrid created by crossing them, 'Granex', the large, sweet strain used for growing the world-famous Vidalia onions.

Recommended Long-Day Onions:
Northern gardeners have a few choices for growing large sweet onions: the original 'Walla Walla Sweet', or a couple of English onions named 'Kelsae Sweet Giant' and 'Ailsa Craig Exhibition'. A storage onion that sweetens over time is the hybrid 'Sweet Sandwich', which is great for salads, but does not cook well. Storage onions for the north are abundant and include longtime favorites, like the 'Southport Globe' series (yellow, white and red), and a lot of new hybrids whose names change as rapidly as the preferences of the farmers who grow them.

A few onion varieties are relatively insensitive to day length and, thus, can be grown over a wide area of the United States. A keeper that fits this category is the hybrid 'Buffalo', which succeeds from fall plantings as far south as the 30th parallel, which is about the northern border of Florida and the U.S.-Mexican border. The sweet variety 'Stockton Red', is also fairly day-length neutral, as are the Italian heirloom, bottle-shaped onions known as 'Florence Red', 'Rossa di Lucca', or simply 'Italian Torpedo'.

---

p

Parsnips

COMMON NAME
Parsnip

BOTANICAL NAME
Pastinaca sativa

RECOMMENDED ZONES (USDA)
ALL

Parsnips have been in general cultivation since the 16th century.

Old-fashioned favorites: parsnips.

Parsnips aren't extremely well-known, yet they are a very old crop by American standards. Parsnip seed was brought over from Europe by the early colonists. They are great in the kitchen because their large white roots have a sweet, yet nutty flavor that is unique in the vegetable world. They are used in soups and stews.

GROWING
Parsnips need a deep, well-prepared soil. They are best grown in a dedicated bed where they can be left undisturbed from early spring until late fall.

Sow as soon as the ground dries in spring, placing the seed a half-inch deep, 20 seeds to the foot in rows at least a foot apart. In rich, loose soil the plants will grow quite large, so thin to a minimum six inches between plants. Keep the soil loose and weeds down.

If you have a hard or tight soil, take an iron digging bar, and every six inches along a prepared furrow, jam it as far into the soil as possible, then rotate the bar to make conical holes. Fill these with sifted compost and sow three seeds in each. When the seedlings sprout, take out all but the strongest one.

HARVESTING
Harvest is in late fall, after a number of freezes, or you can mulch the plants heavily and leave them in the ground until early spring, then dig the roots before regrowth. Most fanciers tell you that spring-dug roots taste better.

PROTECTING
If a few parsley worms appear (see carrots), pick them off and crush them, or relocate them to a place where you don't mind them feeding (they become the black swallowtail butterfly).

CHOOSING THE BEST VARIETIES
The standard varieties of parsnip are 'All-America', 'Hollow Crown', and an

English variety called 'Cobham' or 'Cobham Improved Marrow'.

Peas

COMMON NAMES
Shell Pea, Snow Pea, Chinese Pea, Snap Pea

BOTANICAL NAME
Pisum sativum

RECOMMENDED ZONES (USDA)
ALL

An ancient plant of southern Europe which spread east to India and China,

The popular 'Sugar Snap' pea.

dried peas were a staple crop of the peasantry during the Middle Ages, due to their high protein and carbohydrate content. They remain a staple in cuisines worldwide.

Years ago, peas were peas. Shucked fresh or dried for winter soups and stews, they were nonetheless a single plant, grown and harvested in a single way. No more. Now American gardeners grow three distinct kinds of peas: shelling peas, the standard kind,

whether grown for fresh or dry use; edible pod peas, which are picked before the peas themselves begin to grow and used for salad, crudites and stir fry; and snap peas, in which the entire pea-swollen pod is eaten whole, usually fresh or just lightly steamed. See the recipe for Pear Tomatoes and Snow Peas on page 126.

Some varieties are quite ornamental and can be used on a trellis to form visual structure.

GROWING
Peas need a well-drained soil, and a trellis or fence on which to climb. All three types are grown by the same general method. Sow as soon as the ground can be worked in spring, placing 10 to 15 seeds to the inch, one inch deep, in double rows four inches apart, with at least three feet between pairs. We put one of these double rows down the center of a three-foot-wide raised bed, and sow spinach or some other cool season green in rows along the edges (the greens will be gone by the time pea harvest comes). Before the seedlings appear, erect a trellis for the plants, which climb by holding onto a support with tendrils.

Dwarf varieties can get by with a three-foot-tall structure, but the most

Picking sugar snow peas.

'Green Arrow' peas.

Pruned branches provide support.

Harvest snow peas when young.

vigorous will need eight to 10 feet—be sure to check the varietal description! Some gardeners like poultry netting as a surface for the peas to climb, but we prefer to use untreated twine, strung horizontally at three to six inch intervals up the trellis. For dwarf varieties, fresh cut, branchy brush can be stuck, butt end into the ground, and interlocked along the row. As long as there are not high winds, this will serve to support the peas until harvest.

HARVESTING
Harvest proceeds differently for each of the three types of pea. Regular peas should be picked just as the peas fill

the pod, which can be checked by testing a few; an outward sign is the changing of the pod seam from convex to concave, while the surface of the pod is still shiny. For drying, leave the pods on the plants until thoroughly dry. Older types, like the heirlooms 'Alderman' or 'Tall Telephone', tend to be, as you might guess, vigorous and need substantial trellises. Most gardeners these days grow smaller varieties, many of which are still quite productive despite their size. Some good candidates include 'Maestro', 'Knight', 'Green Arrow', 'Progress' and the especially fine tasting heirloom 'Lincoln'. All these will fit nicely on a trellis four feet tall.

Chinese or snow peas are harvested very young—really any time after the flower falls and the pods begin to grow. Best flavor, though, is when the pod has reached maximum size and the peas inside are just beginning to swell; the pods should be just bumpy but still flat overall. There are any number of good varieties, like 'Oregon Giant', 'Dwarf Gray Sugar', and 'Mammoth Melting Sugar', all of which will fit on a four-foot-tall trellis. Our favorite, because of its lovely lavender flowers and tall vigorous vines, is the French variety 'Carouby de Maussane'. This is a very productive and tasty variety, but needs a tall trellis: six to eight feet is a realistic height.

Snap peas can be harvested at any stage, which is the secret to their quick popularity in American gardens (the first, 'Sugar Snap', won an All America Award when it was introduced). It is a vigorous plant, often growing eight to 10 feet tall. Young, the pods are good for stir fry or stuffing with a bit of herb-garlic cheese. Once the pod swells, they can be eaten fresh, pod and all, or shelled out. In recent years, newer versions of the snap pea have been introduced with smaller vines, three to four feet, which makes fencing much easier. Look for 'Sugar Bon', 'Sugar Ann', 'Super Sugarmel', and 'Cascadia'.

Many a cook's favorite: 'Gypsy' peppers, green and ripe red.

Peppers

COMMON NAMES
Pepper, Sweet Pepper, Hot Pepper, Chili Pepper

BOTANICAL NAME
Capsicum annuum; Capsicum frutescens

RECOMMENDED ZONES (USDA)
ALL

Native to South and Central America with a long tradition worldwide, peppers are now a staple worldwide. The unripe, ripe, or dried fruits of pepper bushes are eaten in a number of ways. Small, spicy peppers are used for seasoning; larger, sweeter kinds are used in salads, grilled, stuffed, baked, stir fried, etc.

See the recipes for Ratatouille and Fresh Hot Salsa, on pages 129 and 132.

There is probably a greater taste range between pepper varieties than between the members of any other group of vegetable plants in American gardens—and for good reason. The large group is made up of two very different types: sweet peppers and hot peppers.

Both are grown the same way. However, for hot peppers to develop their characteristic potency, a relatively long, hot season is necessary, which limits their garden range somewhat.

Some varieties are ornamental and can be grown as small specimens; most are grown in special-purpose beds, as with eggplants.

GROWING
The seed should be started two to three

inches deep, in flats or pots, eight to 12 weeks before the frost-free date. Thin the plants as soon as they touch leaves, until they are two inches apart. Keep them at least 60° F day and night, until the frost-free date, then begin to harden the plants by moving them outside for increasingly longer periods each warm day. Once the weather is fully settled, and all danger of frost is past, they can be planted out in the garden.

Set the plants 18 inches apart each way in a well balanced soil that receives full sun, at the same depth that they were in the container. In cool climate areas, a black plastic mulch will be a significant advantage, as it will warm the soil and advance maturity of the peppers by two weeks or more. In a Zone 4 climate like ours, this can be

'Habenero'—hottest of the hot.

'Super Cayenne' peppers.

More than a peck of peppers!

the difference between getting ripe fruits or not.

HARVESTING

Sweet peppers are often harvested immature, and in fact, that is precisely what green peppers are: immature sweet peppers. Left on the plant, green peppers will mature to yellow, gold, or red; purple peppers, a variation only recently arrived on the American scene, are also immature fruits and will change color to red or a deep chocolate brown at maturity.

Hot peppers are rarely used immature, and they, too, reach a range of colors when left to ripen on the plants. They can be, but should not be—if you want full flavor—harvested until fully ripe. At this stage, they will have developed their full color as well, which may be anywhere along the spectrum from yellow to orange, to red, to violet.

Hot peppers are also useful ornamentals. To make wreaths, the plants should be allowed to stand until the majority of the fruits have ripened. Then, cut the plants off at ground level and hang them to dry further in a dry, airy, but frost-free location. Once the fruits have dried fully (and shriveled somewhat), they can be removed from the plants and used for decoration. In humid climates, this further drying is very important if you don't want the fruits to rot once in an arrangement.

CHOOSING THE BEST VARIETIES

The variety of peppers now available is so great that we can only scratch the surface with a few recommendations. For a standard green pepper (that turns red on maturity), we like the French hybrid 'Vidi'; for super early harvest, however, 'Ace' may be a better bet. The 'Earlibird' series from Stokes Seed (see source listings) offers a wide color range, good disease resistance, and a uniform habit. A few other special colored peppers we have been pleased with are 'Islander', 'Purple Beauty', 'Sweet Chocolate', which is very good for short season areas, and 'Chocolate Beauty'.

Among hot peppers some of our favorites are 'Cayenne', 'Serrano', 'Jalapeno', and the super hot 'Habanero' and 'Thai Hot'. Keep in mind that all hot peppers need a long, warm growing season to develop full flavor. If you'd like to make chili wreaths or ristras, consider 'Paper Dragon' or the 'NuMex' series, which

'Thai Hot' peppers.

'Italian Long' sweet peppers.

has a wide range of red, yellow and orange shades, all with the classic small, pointed fruit type.

Potatoes

COMMON NAMES
Potato, Spud

BOTANICAL NAME
Solanum tuberosum

RECOMMENDED ZONES (USDA)
ALL

'Red Pontiac' potatoes.

Potatoes are a staple crop of Andean civilization that were introduced to Europe by returning explorers. Vast numbers of cultivars of incredible diversity still are available. Home gardeners can grow many more kinds than are available in the market. Potatoes can be baked, fried, grilled, or used in soups or stews. See the recipe for Potato and Leek Soup on page 134.

GROWING
The edible tubers require hilling and are spaced at one foot per plant. Potatoes are one of the few vegetable crops where you simply bury what you don't eat to get the next crop. Potatoes are also one of the vegetable crops that will give you rewards of diversity that far outstrip what the supermarket provides. For the best results, you should buy potatoes that were grown under controlled conditions, especially for

The almost unbelievable 'Purple Peruvian' potato.

planting, called "certified"; that way you can be sure that your planting will be free of the common potato diseases that could be easily carried over from year to year on tubers you save from your own harvest.

Planting potatoes is a bit of work, but certainly no difficulty. Since we plant in raised beds, all that is necessary is to take a shovelful of soil out of the bed every foot in a row down the center of the bed. Cut the potatoes you will be using for seed into pieces that weigh at least an ounce and have at least one "eye", the small depressions on the surface of a potato from which new roots and shoots will grow. Place one piece in the bottom of each of the small holes you've dug, then pull soil from the surrounding bed to cover the "sets".

Within two to three weeks, sprouts

will appear. Once they reach four to six inches, use a hoe to pull soil from the surrounding bed to bank up around the emerging plants. When they reach another six to eight inches above the banked soil, repeat the process, but be sure to only pull the soil up around the plants—don't actually cover any of the leaves, as it is the photosynthesis of the leaves that provides for the growth of the plants. The tubers which you will eventually harvest are actually root offsets, and by banking up the plants, you provide more underground plant stem, that is, root, from which offsets can form.

Once we have "hilled up" the plants a second time, we take spoiled hay (other mulch materials will work just as well, as long as they insulate the soil from the heat of the sun) and put a six

Potato blossoms

Buried treasure: the potato harvest.

inch layer of it along both sides of the row. Potatoes prefer to grow in a frost-free, but cool, climate. The mulch, by cutting out the direct rays of the sun, provides a cool environment in which the tubers can form.

HARVESTING

There is no guaranteed way to tell when tubers have begun to form, so harvest is usually a matter of trial and error. Potatoes don't always flower, but if they do, you can feel around in the hilled soil for tubers after that point. The tiny potatoes you are likely to find at that point are some of the best that you will ever eat. Real harvest will commence once the plant tops begin to turn brown and die down. At that point, remove the shriveled tops, then, after a week, you can dig the tubers; this allows time for any disease or rot bacteria that may have been on the dead tops to die before you bring up the tubers.

Once harvest begins, dig up all the tubers that have formed and let them sit on top of the soil for two or three days so their skins have time to firm up; then collect and move them to a dark, dry and airy place—we use screens propped up on cement blocks in the garage. Let them stay there for another week, as long as they don't freeze. After that, without removing the soil that has dried on the tubers, put the harvest into mesh bags or porous crates (we use milk crates) and store in the root cellar.

CHOOSING THE BEST VARIETIES

Main crop potatoes are very regional in their adaptation, and it is a good idea to stick with what works for your area. Among the specialty types, though, we do have some real favorites. For salad, we like the German fingerling types like 'Russian Banana' or 'Rose Finn Apple'; for boiling, 'Red Cloud' or 'Red Norland', 'Irish Cobbler' and 'Green Mountain' (one of our local varieties here in Vermont); for baking, 'Butte' or 'Norkotah Russet', one of the few

bakers that will do really well in short season areas like ours, or the king of the bakers, 'Russet Burbank'.

If you'd like to try something out of the ordinary, I can heartily recommend 'Purple Peruvian', a small, late variety that sports purple-skinned, purple-fleshed potatoes that will charm any child, because when you mash them, you get purple mashed potatoes! I've never met a kid yet that won't try them.

Pumpkins

COMMON NAMES
Pumpkin; Jack O'Lantern

BOTANICAL NAME
Cucurbita pepo; C. maxima; C. moschata

RECOMMENDED ZONES (USDA)
ALL

Pumpkins are wonderful, albeit ground-swallowing plants. While their fruits are one of the classics of fall harvest and winter storage, the amount of space they require puts them out of

Pumpkins, gourds, and squash make a fantastic seasonal display.

'Rouge Vif D'Etampes' pumpkin.

reach for many gardeners. You can trellis the smaller varieties, though, and, thus, fit them in to a kitchen garden if you really want them.

The range of pumpkin varieties has blossomed in recent years, and instead of just your standard 'Jack O'Lantern', there is a range of varieties from only a few inches across up to huge, 600-pound behemoths.

GROWING

As a technical matter, not all of these are really pumpkins, but to a gardener, that is of little importance. In fact, those oddballs are really winter squashes, and the culture of the two plants is similar. Sow the seed in hills at least six feet apart each way after the frost-free date. Cover them with a floating row cover if cucumber beetles are a problem. Then thin to two to three plants per hill and remove the covers once the plants are growing vigorously. Water well and regularly.

CHOOSING THE BEST VARIETIES

At the small end are varieties like 'Munchkin' and 'Jack Be Little', which are bright orange and squared off, like a cheese box. Despite the diminutive size of the fruits, the vines grow rampantly and total yields can be surprisingly high. This is a good bet for small gardens, if you have a way to trellis the vines so as not to use too much ground. Culinary uses are limited, but these mini-pumpkins are great for ornaments, just like other miniature gourds.

Pie pumpkins like 'Small Sugar' and 'New England Pie' run about

'Small Sugar' pumpkins.

eight to 12 inches across and have tastier flesh than the more ornamental types. Their traditional spherical shape and manageable size make them a great compromise if you have room for only one kind, because they are just large enough to carve for Halloween.

The traditional Jack O'Lantern pumpkins are in the 18 to 24 inch

'Jack Be Little' pumpkins.

diameter range, and are much more variable in shape, allowing lots of creative possibilities for carving. Traditional varieties are 'Connecticut Field' and 'Howden', but there are also new hybrids that have a brighter color and more uniformity. If those characteristics are important to you, try kinds like 'Autumn Gold' or 'Big Autumn'. For real monsters you can grow 'Big Moon', or the world-record holding 'Atlantic Giant'!

Our personal favorite pumpkin, however, is an old French heirloom called 'Rouge Vif D'Etampes', which is bright burnt orange to red, about two feet across, and almost flat, less than a foot high. These fruits are unbelievably ornamental and good for both pies and soups.

Radishes

COMMON NAMES
Radish

BOTANICAL NAME
Raphanus sativus

RECOMMENDED ZONES (USDA)
ALL

Radishes are usually the first crop to be harvested in our kitchen garden, and with the right choice of variety, can be one of the last as well. Their versatility in the garden is bested only at the table, where their color range—from white through pink, red and purple to black, the original cultivated form grown at least since the time of the pyramids in Egypt—and their variety of form helps provide both decorative and nutritional touches for salads and crudite platters.

GROWING
Radishes need a moist, well-drained, loose soil. For the best use of space, plant radishes with carrots.

'Chinese Rose' radish.

Early spring crops of standard radishes can be sown as soon as the ground is ready in spring. Set the seed half an inch deep in rows eight inches apart. Once the plants have their first true leaves, thin to an inch apart. When the tops of the roots become visible pushing up through the soil, begin the harvest by pulling every other root.

To save space, we plant spring radishes in the same row as carrots (which see), thus doubling the productivity of that space. As long as you can keep them growing vigorously, which requires a rich, moist, but well-drained soil and protection from hot dry conditions, new plantings every week or two will provide successive crops.

'Easter Egg' radishes.

'Cherry Belle', 'Snow Belle', 'Plum Purple', 'White Icicle', and 'French Breakfast' radishes.

Fall radishes should be sown about 90 days before the first hard frosts of fall, but not before the summer solstice. The rows should be a foot apart, and the roots thinned to a minimum of four inches apart, as they will grow much larger than spring types.

HARVESTING
Spring and summer radishes are not stored. Fall and winter radishes are stored like other root crops: 80 to 90 percent humidity and 35 to 40° F.

PROTECTING
All radishes may be bothered by flea beetles and root maggots—the same insects that bother the cabbage family plants—but both can be easily controlled with floating row covers.

CHOOSING THE BEST VARIETIES
Good varieties to try include 'French Breakfast', 'Fluo', 'Sparkler', 'Icicle' and 'Snow Belle' (two white kinds), 'Plum Purple', and especially for later plantings, when the weather turns hot, 'Easter Egg', a blend of white, pink, red and purple kinds that holds well.

Though there are many kinds of fall radishes, our favorites are the old 'Chinese Rose', a bulbous pink kind

that stores well and is ready about 60 days after planting, and 'Munich Bier', a large white fall radish that is popular in Europe for slicing to enjoy with cheese, bread and *ja!*, a cold beer.

Rhubarb

COMMON NAME
Rhubarb

BOTANICAL NAME
Rheum rhaponticum

RECOMMENDED ZONES (USDA)
ALL, except extreme south

Often referred to as the pie plant, rhubarb is also used for jams, jellies, syrups, and other desserts. You might say rhubarb is the only vegetable we use as a fruit! It's also very easy to grow.

Like our other garden perennials, asparagus and artichokes, rhubarb will produce for many seasons. Just follow a few simple practices and you'll have fresh, juicy stalks for kitchen use for as long as 10 years. See the recipe for Rhubarb Coffee Cake on page 127.

Originally grown in the fertile Volga River basin, rhubarb prefers cooler

weather, but otherwise is not fussy about soil and is pretty much disease- and pest-free. The only parts of the U.S. it won't do well in are areas where its roots won't freeze for at least a short while. It even does well in part shade, unlike most of our other kitchen vegetables. For this reason, you might plant a bed of rhubarb alongside your asparagus bed, even on the shady side, or you might put it inside a south or west wall or fence. Just remember that it will be there for quite a while.

GROWING
It's best to start rhubarb from container-grown plants or crowns, set just below the soil surface. While rhubarb does well in any decent garden soil, it prefers it slightly acidic—6.0 to 6.5 pH.

Plant crowns in the fall (in milder climates) or early spring. Set the plants about three feet apart. Keep them well-watered throughout the growing season and mulch to keep the soil temperature moderate and the weeds away.

The roots will spread, so help them by incorporating organic matter when you prepare your beds and repeat annually. You can divide the clumps yearly for more production without buying new plants.

HARVESTING
Don't pick any stalks the first year. They need to establish themselves before you can harvest stalks. Once

'Victoria' rhubarb.

they are ready, simply grab a stalk that is at least an inch thick and remove it with a twist and a tug.

Two other rules: 1) *never* eat rhubarb leaves. They contain harmful levels of oxalic acid; 2) Don't let the plants flower and set seed, or they'll lose vigor.

CHOOSING THE BEST VARIETIES

While choices in your local garden center may be limited (but still worth growing), you can obtain crowns from most mail order sources. 'Victoria' is the standard variety; it produces green stalks. Some gardeners prefer the red stalks of 'Valentine' and 'Ruby'. In milder climates 'Cherry' or 'Giant Cherry' are good choices.

S

Salad Greens

COMMON NAMES
Baby Greens, Salad Mix, Mesclun

BOTANICAL NAME
Many species used in combination

RECOMMENDED ZONES (USDA)
all

The National Garden Bureau named 1997 "The Year of the Salad Green", a credit long due to this class of kitchen garden plants. Aside from the most common ingredients like lettuce, chicory and spinach, which are treated individually, there are still an enormous number of other crops that taste great in salads, and that can be easily grown even in small gardens.

GROWING AND CHOOSING THE BEST VARIETIES

Greens need rich soil that is well-drained. They can be grown in special beds or as part of ornamental borders.

The two best ways to classify these plants are by flavor—some are strong flavored and others mild—or by

The classic mesclun mix is both beautiful and flavorful.

seasonal adaptation. We will choose the second, and only mention the first in the course of our discussion.

Arugula *(Eruca sativa)* This piquant Italian green is probably the most popular salad green after lettuce, and it is easy to grow both spring and fall. Sow seed a quarter to a half inch deep in rows six to eight inches apart, as soon as the ground is ready to work in the spring. If flea beetles are a problem in your garden, cover the rows immediately after sowing with a floating row cover. Once the plants reach four to

six inches, harvest by cutting off just above ground level with scissors. For a succession crop, plant every 10 to 14 days until the frost-free date, then again starting three weeks before the onset of cool weather in late summer for fall harvest until hard freezes (25° F or below). There are two forms of arugula: a standard, large-leaf kind and a small-leaf kind called "Rustic" or "Selvatica Arugula" *(Eruca selvatica)*.

Cress *(Lepidium sativum)* This is the tiny, peppery green that is used for sprouting, but it is also a great, fast growing outdoor salad plant. Growing instructions are precisely the same as for arugula, but be sure to harvest promptly, as the plants will run to seed soon after their prime harvest period. If that happens, don't despair, though, as the seed pods are quite decorative; just replant and keep on growing! Again, there are two general forms: a broadleaf form and a curly form, just as with parsley.

Watercress (*Nasturtium officinale*) is not a true cress, but we will discuss it here. As it needs abundant water, start the plants by pressing the seed into the surface of a small pot whose base can sit continuously in a small pan of water. Once the plants have grown to an inch or so, transplant the whole clump to the garden. The best place to grow watercress is near the hose faucet, where it will get a lot of extra water without too much effort. Harvest by cutting individual leaf branches off the plant and leave it to provide more.

Mustard (*Brassica* spp.) Widely grown in southern gardens for boiling greens, mustard also makes an excellent, spicy salad plant when

One of the most distinctive of all the salad greens: arugula.

harvested young. Again, the technique is virtually identical to that for arugula (see above). If you want boiling greens, simply leave the last spring planting to

'Red Giant' mustard greens.

Purslane: not always a weed.

grow and harvest when the leaves reach 12 to 18 inches. Our favorite varieties are a green frilly kind, called 'Fordhook Fancy', the purple Japanese kinds, 'Miike Purple', 'Red Giant' and 'Osaka Purple', and the biennial type called 'Mizuna'. This last is an especially valuable plant, as it can grow quite large without becoming hot or bitter.

Mache (*Valerianella locusta*) This hardy but diminutive plant, usually known in the U.S. as Corn Salad, was a common weed in corn fields in the days before widespread herbicide use, and, thus, supplied a ready harvest of nutritious greens during the season when the garden was dormant. Sow in early spring and late summer, half an inch deep in rows only six inches apart. Unlike the other greens already discussed, you should plant a larger amount, not successions. Though once established, mache will hold in condition right through hot or cold weather, it is erratic in germination at other times. The plants can be harvested anytime after they emerge—even after flowering—yet will be tender and mild. Fall plantings can be held through the entire winter in a cold frame. Our favorite varieties are mostly European heirlooms: 'Coquille de Louviers', which has cupped leaves that hold dressing especially well, the super hardy, productive, round leaved 'd'Etampes', and the heat tolerant Italian strain Piedmonte.

Claytonia (*Claytonia perfoliata*) Another super-hardy, semi-wild plant that can provide an off-season harvest from the cold frame, Claytonia is widely grown in Europe for the winter salad, though it is native to the United States, where it has been long known as Miner's Lettuce. Growing instructions are as for Mache.

Chervil (*Anthriscus cerefolium*) This anise-flavored, feathery-leaved plant is a standard component of the traditional European *Mesclun Provencal*. While it does not grow as fast or run to seed as quickly as arugula, the same planting method can be used. Harvest the leaves at four to six inches and remove the stems before adding to the salad.

Purslane (*Portulaca oleracea*) Every garden, it seems, knows how to grow purslane, even if the gardener doesn't plant it. The more upright, large-leaved, cultivated form can be kept from becoming a weed quite easily. Sow the seed no more than an inch deep every two weeks beginning about two weeks, before the frost free date, continuing until about a month before the first fall frosts. Once the plants reach four to six inches tall, cut them off at ground level and add the juicy, ascerbic sprigs to the salad.

Orach (*Atriplex hortensis*) An old country salad plant, orach is also an outstanding ornamental plant when mature. For salad, sow the seed two to

Red orach.

three inches deep in rows only six inches apart, and harvest when the leaves are only about four inches long. As with Purslane, you can plant successions right through the hot months. If you like, thin one of the plantings to one foot per plant and let them grow. They will reach a good six feet tall and bear large seed heads that are excellent for dried arrangements. The most common orach is red, but there are also green and (near) yellow kinds.

HARVESTING
Salad greens are generally harvested for immediate use. For best quality, harvest them young.

PROTECTING
The main threats to salad greens are: ❶ flea beetles for members of the mustard family: and ❷ aphids, which like them all.
   Control flea beetles with floating row covers; use an insecticidal soap against aphids.

CHOOSING THE BEST VARIETIES
See above.

SPECIAL NOTES
Perhaps the most interesting way to provide a diversity of salad plants from your garden is plant a wild salad plot. This is a section of the garden where you plant a few perennial salad plants, like radicchio, sorrel and Good King Henry (*Chenopodium bonus-hericus*), and let the annual plants, like arugula, cress and the others, run wild and self-sow. Then, when you want a

salad you simply visit the spot and harvest whatever leaves and flowers are available. Other plants already in your garden make excellent additions to a salad mix. Basil, dill and many other herbs can provide both leaves and flowers to liven up a salad, as can nasturtiums. Violas, calendulas, marigolds, daylilies and salvias have edible flowers, as do squashes, beans and peas, just to name a few.

Shallots

COMMON NAME
Shallot

BOTANICAL NAME
Allium cepa, aggregatum group

RECOMMENDED ZONES (USDA)
ALL

Gourmet favorite: shallots.

The origin of shallots is unclear. They have never been found in the wild state, but have been lauded since Biblical times.
   A cook should never be without shallots, and the gardening cook need never be—they are one of the easiest crops in the garden to grow.

GROWING
Shallots are leaf vegetables, despite their look. The bulbs are compressed leaf bases. Fifty square feet will provide plenty for winter kitchen use and leave enough in spring to replant!
   Choose a spot that is rich, well-drained and in full sun. Grow shallots

'Success' shallots.

Shallots are not usually braided. Store in mesh bags in a cool, dry room. Save the best bulbs for replanting the next year.

CHOOSING THE BEST VARIETIES

We plant two Dutch strains called 'Atlantic' and 'Success', but any shallot that pleases you in the kitchen is a good candidate for your own garden, as the same bulb that you would mince and sauté can just as easily be planted to provide more of its kind.

'Indian Summer' spinach.

Spinach

COMMON NAMES
Spinach

BOTANICAL NAME
Spinacia oleracea

RECOMMENDED ZONES (USDA)
ALL

Originally from Asia, spinach was brought to Europe by the Moors around 1,000 years ago. It entered widespread cultivation about 200 years ago. One of the oldest plants in our gardens, spinach was already garden-tested for centuries when the first colonists brought it to North America. Equally delicious steamed, boiled, sautéed or in salads, it is a must for the kitchen garden. There are two general types: smooth-leaved and savoy, in which the leaves are puckered and folded.

See the recipe for Spinach Pie with Phyllo Crust on page 125.

GROWING

Spinach demands a rich, moist, well-drained soil to succeed. Special-purpose beds as small as 20 to 30 square feet can produce an enormous amount of spinach in closely spaced rows that are harvested and replanted frequently.

Spinach won't thrive during prolonged hot periods. You can harvest

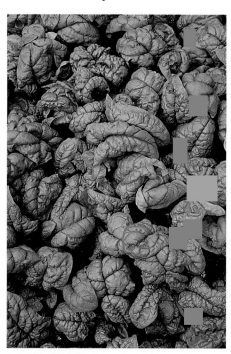

'Tyee' spinach.

in a well-prepared, dedicated bed, like you would with garlic. It is important to remember that, like their relative the onion, shallots are actually a leaf crop and want ample water and nutrients when young; two bushels of compost should provide plenty.

As soon as the ground can be worked in spring, take the shallot bulbs and stick the blunt end into the soil eight to 12 inches apart, so that the narrow pointed end is just below the surface. That's all there is to it!

When the sprouts show, work the soil to keep weeds down. Make sure they get an inch of water a week until the bulbs begin to form, then hold off and let them bulb up and the tops die down (this will be in midsummer).

HARVESTING

Harvest from mid- to late summer. You should get five to 10 times the amount you planted.

Once most of the tops have withered, bend over any slackers, wait two dry days, then pull the crop and leave it on the surface of the soil for two more dry days. Then, move onto screens in a dark, dry place, just as you would for onions or garlic.

Spinach thrives in cool weather.

up to a pound per square foot, more with frequent replantings.

Sow spinach as soon as the ground can be worked in spring, in part to full sun. The seed should be set one-half inch deep, 10 to 15 seeds to the foot, in rows eight to 12 inches apart. Once the plants begin to crowd, thin and use the thinnings for early salads. Later, the plants will increase rapidly in size and can be used for steaming as well as salads.

Fall crops can be planted any time after about August 10, as by then the days are noticeably shorter, and even the last of the summer heat is unlikely to lead to bolting. Once the weather cools down for good, spinach will hold quite well, as long as there is not persistent rain and waterlogged soil. This can lead to problems with mildew.

Continue to plant every week or so until the arrival of hard frost. The harvest will carry you through much of the fall and early winter in all but the coldest and wettest climates.

PROTECTING

The major insect pest we have seen is leaf miners, which attack both beets and spinach on occasion. A floating row cover will exclude the fly that causes the problem, but if you see tunnels in the leaves, you can prevent future infestations by removing the affected leaves and tossing them into the chicken yard or the fire—either way the larvae will be destroyed.

CHOOSING THE BEST VARIETIES

Because many varieties run to seed quickly as the days lengthen in late spring, choose a long-standing variety like the hybrid savoy 'Tyee', or smooth-leaved 'Space'. We used to grow a non-hybrid smooth leaf variety from Holland called 'Estivato', but it is no longer available (though we hope to bring it back over time). Another savoy we have had good, season-long success with is the hybrid 'Indian Summer'.

'Sunburst' scallop', Yellow Straightneck', and 'Seneca' zucchini.

Squash, Summer

COMMON NAMES
Summer Squash

BOTANICAL NAME
Cucurbita pepo

RECOMMENDED ZONES (USDA)
ALL

One of the traditional "three sisters" of the Americas—maize, beans and squashes—they have been cultivated here so long that they're no longer known to exist in the wild.

Some gardeners with memories of a "zucchini glut" dismiss all summer squashes as space-hogging, overpro-ducing garden monsters, but to the cook, a well-managed patch of summer squashes can be a consistent source of gourmet delicacies. See the recipes for Zucchini Phyllo Pizza, and for Squash and Carrot Soup, on pages 132.

There are a wide variety of squashes, although they fall into just a few categories. This diversity, combined with our planting scheme and a couple of dozen square feet (plus an iron resolve at harvest time) is all it takes.

'Ronde de Nice' zucchini.

'Sundance' crookneck.

GROWING

Squash is usually sown in "hills" (described under cucumbers). For squashes, space the hills four to six feet apart, and place eight to 12 seeds in each hill after the ground is fully warmed up and the danger of frost is past. The secret to our planting method is simple: we mix the seeds of three or four kinds in the same hill, and when the plants emerge use scissors to cut off all but six, leaving a range of types (the leaves of each variety are noticeably different). We only plant two or three hills because summer squashes grow as bushes (actually just very compact, nearly upright vines); two or three hills won't take an enormous amount of space.

HARVESTING

Once the plants begin to flower, you will notice that there are both male and female flowers. You can recognize male blossoms because they are held at the end of a slender stem, whereas the female flowers have a thickened ovary at the base. If you look closely, you'll see that the ovaries have the shape and color of the fruits they will become after pollination. Occasionally some female flowers will appear before the males, in which case the ovaries will wither and die, unfertilized. Don't worry! Once the males come along, things will proceed nicely.

The second key element of our squash routine is to harvest young: from as soon as the flowers open until the fruits are up to six inches long, no longer. The tiny fruits with flowers attached are known as "courgettes" in France, and considered a great delicacy. If you harvest your summer squash at this stage, from a mixed planting, I guarantee that you will never have a zucchini glut. On the other hand, your family will never get ahead of the 12 to 18 plants in the hills. More importantly, never let the fruits get bigger than eight inches, or the plants will decrease their production. If you don't need them in the kitchen, cut the fruits off anyway and give them away with a quick story

Leave plenty of room for squash!

about the price of "courgettes" in the market, and you'll find doors opening, not closing, as you work your way down the block with such an "exotic" harvest!

PROTECTING

If cucumber beetles are around, cover the hills with a floating row cover immediately after sowing, and don't remove them until thinning time. A problem just as important in warm climates is the squash borer, which can ruin a planting by mid-summer; the trick for them is to replant a month after the first sowing, so that once they show up in the first planting, you can remove the plants and destroy them along with the larvae. Then, let the second planting come along until frost kills the plants.

CHOOSING THE BEST VARIETIES

There are crookneck squashes: yellow, bulbous at one end, with a thin, curved neck. Our favorite of these is called 'Sundance'. There are straight yellow kinds with one end fatter than the other, like 'Sunbar', and usually cylindrical kinds (the true zucchini), which come in a range of colors from bright gold ('Gold Rush') through pale ('Greyzini') and medium green ('Milano') to almost black ('Black Jack'), though some are slightly bulbous ('Ghada') or even spherical ('Ronde de Nice' zucchini). Then there are Patty Pan kinds in both gold ('Sunburst') and shades of green ('Bennings Green Tint' or 'Scallopini').

Squash, Winter

COMMON NAME
Winter Squash

BOTANICAL NAME
Cucurbita pepo; C. maxima; C. moschata

RECOMMENDED ZONES (USDA)
ALL

'Scallopini' summer squash.

'Greyzini' male and female flowers.

A collection of winter squash, ready for use through the cold season.

green, are also members of the species *C. pepo*, but have slightly longer vines; because of their convenient size and great flavor, though, they are among some of our personal favorites.

Butternut squashes are from a different species (*C. moschata*) and bear tan, smooth-skinned fruits shaped like a barbell. They need a good bit of space, but the five-pound fruits store longer than most others, and are resistant to vine borers (see Summer Squash). The flesh is sweet and moist, and makes an excellent soup when combined with carrots (see the recipe for Squash and Carrot Soup on page 132).

The species *Cucurbita maxima* includes the five-pound and under, blocky, dark green "Buttercup" squashes, the similar-sized Japanese "Kabocha" and brightly colored "Hokkaido" types, as well as the classic giant blue-gray and green "Hubbard" squashes that are heaped in near mountains around country farm stands in the fall. These are all vigorous, rambling plants and are probably best left to the farmers and market gardeners, unless you have *plenty* of room.

Winter squashes are even more diverse than summer kinds. The acorn squashes are members of the same species, bear two-pound fruits that will keep two to three months, and ramble only slightly more than summer types. They are good for larger gardens.

GROWING

Except for the fact that they need more room, winter squashes are grown in the same manner as summer squashes. The seed should be sown in hills at least six feet apart each way after the frost-free date; covered with a floating row cover if cucumber beetles are a problem, and then thinned to two to three plants per hill once the plants are growing vigorously.

CHOOSING THE BEST VARIETIES

Among the Acorn squashes, you can grow dark green varieties like 'Table Ace' and 'Ebony Acorn', the bright 'Table Gold', or even white-fruited varieties like 'Cream of the Crop' or

'Swan White Acorn'. The so-called "Sweet Potato" squashes, which have small pound-and-a-half fruits with pale-ivory skin, furrowed with dark

'Kabocha' and 'Red Kure' squash.

'Blue Hubbard' squash.

'Early Butternut' squash.

'Acorn' squash.

An autumn menagerie of pumpkins and winter squash.

HARVESTING

Winter squashes, like pumpkins, should be left on the plant until the vines wither and die in late summer to early fall. If they are mature enough to store, light frosts will not hurt them, though they should be covered if the frost will be significant. You can tell when they have reached this stage (and are ready to harvest) by trying to nick the rind of the fruits with your fingernail. Those that are not easily marked are ready; cut them with an inch of stem remaining and gather in the garden, so they can be covered conveniently. Cure in the sun for a week, gather and dunk in a ratio of 10-to-1 water-to-bleach solution to kill bacteria on the surface, then store in a cool (45 to 50° F), dry location for the winter.

....

t

Tomatillos

COMMON NAME
Tomatillo

BOTANICAL NAME
Physalis ixocarpa

RECOMMENDED ZONES (USDA)
ALL

Tomatillos are native to South America, but now widely naturalized in Central America, Africa, Europe and even Australia.

With the increasing popularity of Latin American food, the tomatillo is becoming more widely grown. It is essential for an authentic Salsa. Nothing could be easier to grow, either.

See the recipe for Fresh Hot Salsa on page 132.

GROWING

Tomatillos grow well in any garden soil. Grow a few plants in the tomato bed for convenience of culture.

Start the seed indoors a month before the frost-free date and set out in the garden after the danger of frost is past, with a spacing of 18 to 24 inches per plant. The bushy plants grow fast, and will soon bear small one to two

'Orange Hubbard' squash.

'Table Gold' squash.

Ripe tomatillos.

Tomatillos are prolific bearers.

inch, tomato-like fruits encased in "paper lanterns".

HARVESTING
Once the lanterns start to fade, and then open at the tip, pick the green, slightly sticky fruits. They can be used fresh, in salads, or added to salsa.

Tomatoes

COMMON NAME
Tomato

BOTANICAL NAME
Lycopersicon esculentum

RECOMMENDED ZONES (USDA)
ALL

The tomato has an illustrious history in the garden, first as an ornamental, then as a reputed aphrodisiac, and now as America's favorite garden vegetable.

Despite a long history as a garden plant, tomatoes were at first thought to be poisonous, and only came into the vegetable garden in the mid 1800s. Today, however, they are the single most popular vegetable (fruit, actually) grown in American gardens. Well grown, vine-ripened tomatoes are considered along with sweet corn and melons, the pinnacle of the vegetable gardener's art.

In the post-World War II period, tomato breeders worked feverishly to develop a broad range of new, mostly hybrid tomato varieties that incorporated high and uniform yields with increased disease resistance. The most popular varieties in the '70s and '80s, well-known names like 'Early Girl', 'Big Boy', 'Supersonic', 'Celebrity', 'Jetstar' and 'Whopper', were the hot items in every seed catalog's list.

Over the past decade or so this has changed somewhat, and American gardeners seem to have a fascination for old-fashioned tomatoes, called heirlooms, with names like 'Brandywine', 'Big Rainbow', 'White Wonder', 'Purple Calabash' and 'Evergreen'. Yes, none of these is your standard, round, red, hopelessly perfect tomato, and all of them were saved from near extinction by a cadre of collectors around the country whose passion has now spread back into the mainstream. That many heirlooms don't yield as well, sometimes have malformed fruits and can succumb to various diseases before reaching their prime, has not kept gardeners from growing them. Their superior flavor and wonderfully diverse appearance are too central to what draws cooks and connoisseurs to kitchen gardening: the search for unique and interesting ingredients.

See the recipes for Rainbow Tomatoes; Ratatouille; Pear Tomatoes and Snow Peas, and Fresh Hot Salsa on pages 126, 129, 130, and 132.

GROWING
From a use perspective, there are three types of tomatoes: ❶ slicing tomatoes, ❷ cherry tomatoes, and ❸ the drier, meatier paste tomatoes. All are grown

What every gardener waits all year for: a bumper crop of tomatoes.

*U*nlike commercial tomatoes, which are picked while they are still green, the home gardener has the luxury of allowing their tomatoes develop their full vine-ripened perfection.

'Striped German' tomatoes.

'Early Girl' tomatoes.

the same, depending on which of the two cultural groups they fall into, determinate or indeterminate: Determinate plants stop growing at a certain point; indetermiate ones continue to vine and will need taller trellising.

Tomatoes are actually a perennial tropical vine that temperate zone gardeners grow as an annual. As such, most tomatoes will continue to grow, sprouting new stems from each leaf axil (the junction of a leafy branch with the main stem) until killed by frost.

Early in the 20th century, an attentive grower spotted a mutant plant in a field of tomatoes, one that grew only to a few feet tall and then stopped. He saved the seeds and over time, breeders crossed them with the vining kinds to produce strains that have a more restrained habit.

This is crucial to commercial growers, but also matters to kitchen gardeners, because it affects how big a trellis—a must for home gardeners— will be needed to support the plants and keep the fruits off the ground. It affects harvest period too.

Tomatoes should be started indoors eight to 10 weeks before the last frost in your area. Sow the seed one-half

inch deep in flats or around the edges of pots, and set the containers in a warm place to germinate. Tomatoes sprout best at 75 to 85° F, so if you don't have a heating mat, put them in the furnace room or on top of the refrigerator. Once the sprouts appear, move them immediately to a place with the brightest possible light; at

'Sweet William' tomatoes.

transplant time, you want stocky plants that are as tall as they are wide. Without full sun, the seedlings will begin to stretch and become weak and spindly. Avoid over-fertilizing or raising the temperature to push the plants along. Both these changes will only make things worse; the only solution for spindly plants is to change the relation between light and temperature as noted in chapter 3.

As soon as the first true leaves appear (the serrated ones), snip off any excess plants, so that the leaves of the seedlings are not quite touching. From this point on try to keep the plants at 65° F in the daytime and 55° F at night. This is ideal for early fruiting and stocky growth, but don't worry if you can't hit this goal exactly. Each time the plants become crowded, move them to larger quarters and, in the process, set them a little deeper than they were in their last home. This encourages growth of extra feeder roots from the lower part of the stem. By transplant time, you'll need a minimum of four inches square per plant. Six to eight inches would be even better if you can provide it.

Once the frost-free date arrives,

'Sun Gold' cherry tomatoes.

'Jetstar' tomatoes with 'Flat-leaved Italian' parsley.

harden the plants off gradually over a week or so, then set them out in the garden on a dull, overcast and preferably still day, preceding a warm rain. If these conditions aren't imminent, simply water the plants well after setting. We use a spacing of two feet apart in double rows that are themselves two feet apart. In a 30-inch raised bed, this amounts to two parallel rows eight inches in from the edge, with a plant every two feet. This is an intense planting, but as long as the soil has been well amended with compost and manure, the plants will thrive in full sun. If your summer rains are inconsistent, like ours, lay a piece

of drip or ooze irrigation tubing between the rows to supply water later in the season (tomatoes do better if you can avoid overhead watering).

The trellises should be set up as soon as practical after transplanting to

'Brandywine' tomatoes.

minimize later disturbance of the plants. For determinate tomatoes, we use sections of wire mesh that contractors use to reinforce concrete floors (it is sold at building materials stores), which has a grid of solid, eight gauge wires with a six to seven inch spacing —large enough to reach through for easy harvesting. We cut a five-by-five foot section of this wire and remove the outermost cross wires, so that we end up with six-inch wire "legs" on two sides. Since the wire retains the curve of the roll it was on after cutting, we end up with a small Quonset frame with legs. It is a simple matter to lay it over the row lengthwise along the bed, and set the legs into the soil to anchor it. The plants then grow up through the mesh and bear the majority of their fruit on top of it, safer from soil rots and hungry rodents. Three pairs, that is six plants, will fit within each Quonset, and the structure can be extended as far as you like. In Spain, this method is used for literally hundreds of acres of commercial tomatoes. We have found it quite efficient and yet, still aesthetic, which is one of our requirements.

For the indeterminate tomatoes, we use a larger trellis. Once the plants and irrigation tuding are set, stick an eight-foot pole loosely into the ground on the edge of the bed, just outside each plant. We use bamboo for its aesthetic beauty, but two by two lumber, or even rough cut saplings, will work just as well. Bind the tops of two pair of poles with twine about a foot down from the top above the center of the bed between the rows, so that you have a

'Evergreen' tomatoes.

'White Beauty' tomatoes.

'Calabash' tomatoes.

series of four legged teepees. Along the top of this phalanx of teepees, we run a horizontal member and lash it down to each, so that the whole unit is solid. We learned about this system on a visit to Bermuda, where high winds are a problem for tomato growers. It makes, without a doubt, the most wind resistant trellis I have seen.

A couple of weeks later, once the sun has had a chance to thoroughly warm the soil, we cultivate the tomatoes, then lay down a six- to eight-inch-thick mulch of hay or straw to hold moisture and to protect the tomato plants from disease spores in the soil that would otherwise be splashed onto their leaves by the rain. We have found that near complete prevention of blight—one of the scourges of humid-climate tomato growers— can be achieved by this simple preventive method. It is critical, however, that absolutely no soil be visible, as even a pinch of soil holds enough bacteria to infect the crop! From this point on the determinate tomatoes will require no further care unless problems arise.

As the indeterminate tomatoes grow, tie each plant to its pole, once for

each flower cluster—you'll see them arising from the main stem alternately with leafy branches—and remove all of the sprouts in the axils above the leafy branches for the first two feet above the ground, as soon as they appear. This tying and pruning will provide an airy layer close to the ground that will increase your protection from soil-borne bacteria and fungi.

From two feet on up to the top of the trellis, less attention is necessary. Simply tie a string to one corner leg of the teepee (or row of teepees), wrap the twine around the next leg in line twice, then continue to the next leg and the next, down the entire row of teepees, around the end, and back the other side in the same fashion. Do this every foot or so up the legs of the teepee(s) and you will have created a grid on which the plants will grow out through and drape. The beauty of this system is that, as the tomatoes weigh down the string, it moves down the diverging legs, tightening itself as it goes!

HARVESTING

Most determinate tomatoes tend to ripen their fruit all at once, and, thus,

we grow them mostly for processing into paste and sauce (though super early determinate tomatoes can be grown under a tunnel to move harvest forward a few weeks). Their flavor is never as good as the more vigorous kinds, however, and so we stick with indeterminates for slicing and cherry types.

Harvest when the fruits are fully ripe. We all know the proper color for a red tomato, but for "white" tomatoes, wait until they turn an ivory color; yellow tomatoes should be gold; green tomatoes a warm olive color and purple tomatoes, burgundy to almost brown. After harvest, store (if at all) at room temperature. Refrigeration ruins the flavor of tomatoes.

PROTECTING

Yellowing foliage may indicate nutrient deficiencies, which can be cured by side dressing or foliar feeding with a fish- or seaweed-based fertilizer, used according to the label recommendations. Tomato hornworms and Colorado potato beetles can both be controlled by hand picking or by use of Bt (*Bacillus thuringiensis*) sprays.

Turnips

COMMON NAMES
Turnip

BOTANICAL NAME
Brassica rapa

RECOMMENDED ZONE (USDA)
ALL

The turnip and its close relative, the rutabaga, have been a staple food in Europe since prehistoric times. Like the parsnip, turnips declined in popularity with the introduction of the potato from the New World. They are used in soups and stews.

'Purple Top' spring turnips.

GROWING

Turnips need a moderately fertile, well-drained soil that has not been home to a cabbage family member the previous year. As with radishes, they are best grown in conjunction with beets and carrots in production beds. Space them similar to beets—about four to six inches apart for high production.

HARVESTING

Harvest spring through late fall; winter in milder climates. Yield should be two to five pounds per square foot.

CHOOSING THE BEST VARIETIES

For spring turnips, we suggest 'Market Express' or 'Purple Top' types, while for fall turnips (rutabagas), we suggest 'Gilfeather'.

Chapter 5

SEASONAL RECIPES FOR THE KITCHEN GARDEN

SPRING

Arugula Salad

Ingredients
1 tablespoon wine vinegar
1 teaspoon Dijon mustard
1 clove garlic, minced
4 tablespoons virgin olive oil
2 cups mixed baby lettuce
1 cup arugula

Instructions
In a wooden salad bowl, whisk together vinegar, mustard, and garlic. Add oil in a slow, steady stream, whisking until well blended. Allow dressing to stand in bowl for five to 10 minutes for flavors to blend.

Meanwhile, wash lettuce and arugula; dry leaves. Make sure all moisture is removed, or dressing will not coat leaves. Add greens to salad bowl, toss and serve.

Serves 4

Opposite *There's simply no comparison between store-bought salad greens and homegrown specialities like arugula and baby lettuce.*

Spinach Pie with Phyllo Crust

Ingredients
2 tablespoons oil
2 tablespoons butter
1 sweet onion, peeled and chopped
8 cups spinach (savoy or flat-leafed), washed
3 eggs
½ cup cottage cheese
¼ teaspoon freshly grated nutmeg
½ package phyllo dough, left at room temperature to defrost
½ cup unsalted butter

Instructions
Preheat oven to 375° F Heat oil and butter in a skillet large enough to hold spinach. Over medium heat, sauté onion until golden (three to five minutes). Add spinach to pan with water still clinging from the washing and cook over medium heat until spinach is reduced and cooked. Cover pan to encourage quick steaming of spinach. Remove lid, and continue to cook spinach a few more minutes until most of the moisture from cooking has been absorbed (10 to 15 minutes). Meanwhile, beat eggs until frothy in a food processor. Add spinach to eggs and quickly chop . Blend in cottage cheese and nutmeg. Transfer to a bowl and set aside. In a small saucepan, melt butter. Prepare phyllo as per instructions on box. Using a pastry brush, paint the inside of an open square casserole dish (approximately 3 inches deep by 12 inches long by 8 inches wide). Place two sheets of phyllo in the pan, using the pastry brush, sparingly coat top layer

with melted butter. Repeat this process eight times. Pour in spinach filling. Place two sheets of phyllo on top of filling and repeat buttering and bread crumbs process eight more times. Place in the oven and bake for 30 to 40 minutes until top turns a golden brown. Serve warm, although equally good cold the next day with a luncheon salad.

Serves 6

Asparagus Crepes

Ingredients
24 medium-sized stalks fresh asparagus
½ lb. grated Swiss cheese
12 crepes (extra-thin pancakes. Recipes abound in classic French cookbooks)
butter for pan

Instructions
Rinse and trim asparagus stalks with a vegetable peeler to remove tough lower stalk and to make an even length, about seven inches. In shallow saucepan, place asparagus in a single layer and add water. Bring to a boil and gently simmer five to eight minutes until the asparagus is tender, yet still firm. Drain and cut stalks in half.

Set up a work area, with the bowl of grated cheese, the asparagus, and the crepes. Begin by placing a small amount of cheese in the center of a crepe. Lay four or five pieces of

An elegant appetizer or vegetarian main course, asparagus crepes are finished off with a bit the classic béchamel sauce.

asparagus on top of it. Fold over the ends, and then roll up the crepe as you would an egg roll, forming a rectangle about four inches long by two inches wide. Place rolled crepes in a buttered shallow casserole. Heat in a low oven until they are warmed through and the cheese has melted. Or heat on stove top in a skillet over a low flame. Serve with béchamel sauce, seasoned with lemon rind and cucumber or a spicy salsa.

Serves 2 to 4 (side dish)

Pear Tomatoes and Snow Peas Stuffed with Herb-Garlic Cheese

Ingredients
Herb-Garlic Cheese
8 ounce package of cream cheese
2 tablespoons softened butter
2 cloves garlic, peeled and minced
1 tablespoon fresh basil, chopped
1 tablespoon fresh dill, minced
1 tablespoon fresh chives, chopped
6 pitted black olives (optional)

Vegetables
1 pint yellow pear or cherry tomatoes
1 pint red pear or cherry tomatoes
½ pound snow peas, stems removed and strings discarded

Instructions
To make Herb-Garlic Cheese Blend cream cheese, butter, garlic and herbs in a food processor or blender until smooth, scraping down sides as necessary. Add olives, if used, and blend again briefly until combined.

To prepare vegetables Remove a third off the top of each tomato. Carefully scoop out seeds and invert tomatoes on a paper towel. Steam snow peas briefly to tenderize, if desired. Split peas down the string side, keeping the two parts connected by the other seam. Fill tomatoes and snow peas with Herb-garlic cheese. Arrange on a decorative plate so that the peas overlap around the edge. Alternate the red and yellow tomatoes in the center.

Serves 8 to 10 (appetizer)

Spring Greens Soup

Ingredients
6 scallions, trimmed & chopped (½ cup)
2 tablespoons butter

2 tablespoons oil
2 medium-sized potatoes, peeled and diced (2 cups)
2 cups homemade broth—chicken or vegetable
2 cups sorrel or spinach greens
1 cup watercress, garden cress or Arugula
1 cup lettuce

Instructions

Sauté the onions in the butter and oil until soft. Stir in the potatoes, cook one to two minutes then add one cup broth. Cover and simmer over medium heat 15 minutes, until potatoes are almost soft. Wash greens, and tear into small pieces or chiffonade with a knife. Add to the soup pot, simmer five minutes, stir and test the potatoes again, this time they should be very soft. Puree in a blender or food processor. Return to the pot, add the remaining one cup of stock and simmer for a few minutes. Serve hot and garnish with snipped chives.

Serves 4

Rhubarb Coffee Cake

Ingredients
½ cup butter
1 ½ cups brown sugar
1 egg
1 cup whole wheat flour

Everyone knows about rhubarb pie, but have you heard of a rhubarb coffee cake? A perfect finale for a spring feast.

1 cup unbleached white flour
1 tsp. baking soda
½ tsp. salt
1 cup sour cream
1 ½ cups rhubarb, cut into ½ inch pieces
½ cup chopped walnuts or pecans

Topping
½ cup butter
1 cup sugar
½ cup light cream
1 tsp. vanilla

Instructions

Preheat oven to 350° F. Cream together butter, brown sugar and egg until light and fluffy. Combine flours, baking soda and salt. Add to creamed mixture alternately with sour cream, mixing well after each addition. Stir in rhubarb and nuts. Spoon into well-greased 9" x 13" cake pan. Bake for 35–40 minutes. Remove from oven and cool.

To make topping, combine butter, sugar, cream and vanilla in small saucepan. Heat until butter melts, then pour over cake.

Makes one cake

SUMMER

Zucchini Phyllo Pizza

Ingredients
2 tablespoons butter
2 tablespoons oil
½ package phyllo dough (defrost according to directions on package)
1 small green zucchini
1 small yellow summer squash
½ cup Parmesan cheese, freshly grated
¼ cup mixed fresh herbs—savory, thyme, parsley and basil
⅛ cup wheat germ
½ sweet red onion, thinly sliced

Instructions

Preheat oven to 400° F. In a small saucepan, heat the butter and oil until butter has melted. Remove from the heat. Thinly slice the zucchini and set aside. Place herbs in a bowl

Opposite Zucchini phyllo pizza is another excellent vegetarian creation, featuring a bounty of summer produce, fresh from the garden.

and finely snip with scissors (or chop on a cutting board). Combine herbs and grated cheese and set aside.

Remove phyllo from the package, place on the counter. Using a pastry brush, lightly oil a cookie sheet or 9-inch pie pan with melted butter and oil. Place two sheets of phyllo on the cookie sheet. Brush it lightly with the melted oil and butter. Sprinkle with approximately 2 tablespoons of the fresh herbs and cheese, then press down lightly. Butter, sprinkle, and layer in the same manner six times until 12 sheets of phyllo have been used. (Roll up the remaining phyllo, wrap in plastic wrap and refreeze for another time.)

Sprinkle the top layer with thin slices of onion and the zucchini. Alternate colors of green and yellow zucchini by lining the slices in tight rows. Sprinkle with remaining cheese and herbs. Curl up the edges of the phyllo and brush whole pizza with remaining oil. Bake for 15 to 20 minutes. Remove to cooling rack; cut into squares or wedges.

Serves 4–8 (appetizer)

Ratatouille

Ingredients
⅓ cup olive oil
2 cloves garlic, peeled & chopped
1 large onion, chopped
3 tablespoons flour
1 zucchini, cut into ¼ inch chunks
1 eggplant, peeled and cubed
2 green peppers, cut into strips
5 tomatoes, coarsely chopped
1 tablespoon each chopped fresh basil and oregano
1 tablespoon capers or nasturtium buds

Instructions
Heat oil in a large skillet. Add garlic and onions and sauté until transparent. Place flour in a plastic bag. Add squash and egg-plant, close bag and shake gently to coat pieces. Add squash, eggplant and peppers to skillet. Cook, uncovered, over low heat for one hour, stirring occasionally. Add tomatoes and herbs and simmer, uncovered, until mixture is thick. Add capers or nasturtium buds during last 15 minutes of cooking. Serve hot or cold.

Serves 6

Cucumber & Lemon Salad

Ingredients
1 lemon
4 cucumbers
1 sweet red pepper
salt
⅛ cup chopped parsley
½ cup olive oil
⅛ cup lemon juice

Instructions
Cut lemon in half (with skin still intact) and then into thin slices. Cut these thin slices into triangles. Place in a glass bowl and sprinkle generously with course salt. Allow to sit 30 minutes. (The salt takes the bitterness out of the skin.)

Slice cucumbers into thin one-eighth-inch pieces. Thinly slice the red pepper. Combine the cucumbers, peppers, parsley and the lemons in a nice bowl. Dress with olive oil, lemon juice and another sprinkling of salt. Leave at room temperature until ready to serve.

Serves 4 (side dish)

Simple and refreshing, cucumber and lemon salad is a summer favorite, especially good paired with spicy dishes.

Cornichons

Ingredients
3 cups (Cornichons) cucumbers
3 tablespoons kosher salt
5 sprigs of fresh tarragon
½ teaspoon mustard seeds
White wine vinegar

Instructions
Wash the cucumbers, rubbing the sharp spines off the skin. Pat dry. In a ceramic or glass bowl, place cucumbers with the salt and mix well. Allow to stand for 24 hours. Drain the juice and again pat the cucumbers dry. Place in a large glass crock or canning jar, leaving a two-inch space from the top, and add the tarragon, the mustard seeds and top with wine vinegar, poured at least one inch above the tops of the cucumbers. Cover the jar and leave in the refrigerator for four weeks.

Pickle as you go along, remove cured pickles for salads and eating, and add new cucumbers that have been salted and drained and towel-dried.

Raspberry vinaigrette

Ingredients
2 heads baby Romaine lettuce
⅓ cup walnut oil
3 tablespoons raspberry vinegar

Instructions
Slice romaine lettuce heads in half. Place on plate. Garnish edges with edible flowers, apple slices or sprigs of fresh herbs. In a small bowl, whisk together oil and vinegar and drizzle over lettuce before serving.

Serves 2 to 4

Fruit Salad with Lemon Balm

Ingredients
6 to 8 cups of mixed summer berries, five different kinds
¼ cup lemon balm leaves, finely chopped
¼ to ½ cup sugar

Instructions
Wash and trim the berries. Place in a glass bowl. Sprinkle with lemon balm and ¼ cup sugar. Put in the refrigerator

The luscious flavor of berries fresh from the garden need little enhancement, just a simple dressing of lemon balm and sugar.

until ready to use. If desired, stir in remaining ¼ cup of sugar.

Serves 4 to 6

Rainbow Tomatoes

Ingredients
4 large ripe tomatoes—mix varieties for a range of colors and flavors.
¼ cup fine green basil leaves, plucked from the stem
3 tablespoons olive oil
2 tablespoons fresh lemon juice
1 teaspoon sugar
salt and freshly ground pepper to taste

Instructions
Cut tomatoes into wedges. Arrange on a platter in a single layer. Sprinkle evenly with basil leaves. In a small bowl, mix together remaining ingredients. Pour over tomatoes and allow to stand at room temperature for one hour before serving.

Serves 2

FALL

Broccoli with Cheese

Ingredients
1 head fresh broccoli
3 tablespoons butter
1 tablespoon flour
1 cup milk
½ cup grated cheddar cheese
1 tablespoon olive oil
1 clove garlic, peeled and diced
½ cup cubed whole wheat bread

Instructions
Preheat oven to 350° F. Cut broccoli into good sized florets and steam for 2 minutes. With 1 tablespoon butter, coat the inside of a gratin dish and arrange broccoli in a single layer. In a saucepan over lowest heat, melt 2 tablespoons butter; stir in the flour until blended. Slowly stir in the milk and grated cheese until smooth and thick. Pour over broccoli. In a skillet, heat olive oil and garlic. Brown bread cubes until crispy. Distribute over broccoli and sauce. Bake 20 minutes or until heated.

Fried Fennel (Finnochio)

Ingredients
2 fennel bulbs
1 egg
1 cup bread crumbs
oil—for frying
coarse sea salt

Instructions
Trim fennel bulb by removing the stems and feathery leaves. (Set aside for another use.) Holding fennel bulb root side down, slice vertically into one-quarter-inch thick slices. Drop into boiling water for three to five minutes, until soft. In a bowl, beat egg. Set up a work station with the beaten egg and the bread crumbs in separate bowls. Dip a slice of fennel into the egg, then into the bread crumbs, lightly tamp down so both sides are coated. Set aside.

With its mild licorice flavor and snappy texture, fried fennel is a perfect accompaniment for a fresh fish entree of any type.

Meanwhile, heat oil to frying temperature (350° F). Drop fennel into hot oil, cook a minute until golden, flip and cook the other side until golden and remove to paper towel or drain. Repeat until all the fennel has been fried. Set onto a serving plate; sprinkle with coarse salt. Serve warm.

Baked Chard

Ingredients
12 to 16 chard stems
salt
½ cup freshly grated Parmesan cheese
4 tablespoons butter

Instructions
Trim green leaves from the chard stems. (Reserve for steaming or sautéing another day.) Remove strings and trim top and bottom off the chard. Place chard stems in boiling, salted water. Cook until soft and tender, 15 minutes. Drain.

Preheat oven to 400° F. Butter a shallow casserole. Spread out a single layer of chard in the casserole. Sprinkle with salt, then half the Parmesan cheese to cover. Add another layer of chard and sprinkle with remaining cheese. Dot with butter. Bake until brown and crusty, about 20 minutes.

Serves 4 (side dish)

A heartwarming fall favorite, squash and carrot soup is mildly spiced with ginger, turmeric, cumin, and cinnamon.

Squash and Carrot Soup

Ingredients
2 tablespoons each, safflower oil & butter
1 clove garlic (or shallots), minced
1 tablespoon crystallized ginger, chopped
⅛ teaspoon each turmeric, cumin, cinnamon
8 carrots, rinsed & sliced
3 cups butternut squash, cut into one-inch cubes
5 cups water
½ cup cider

Instructions
In a four-quart stock pot, heat oil and butter over medium heat. Sauté garlic (or shallots) until golden. Add the ginger and spice; cook for two minutes. Stir in carrots and squash; cook for four minutes. Add water and cider, then cover. Allow soup to simmer for 45 minutes, stirring occasionally, until carrots and squash are soft. Remove from heat, and puree in food processor or blender until smooth. Return to the stock pot. Reheat and serve warm.

Peach Chutney

Ingredients
3 cups dark brown sugar
2 cups cider vinegar

Opposite *Peach chutney and fresh hot salsa are preserved reminders of the summer garden and make wonderful gifts for the winter holidays.*

2 tablespoons chili powder
1 tablespoon salt
2 tablespoons mustard seed
1 onion, thinly sized (½ cup)
1 cup ginger, crystallized, snipped into small pieces
5 pounds fresh ripe peaches

Instructions
In a large kettle, mix together sugar and vinegar and bring to a boiling point. Stir until sugar has dissolved. Add remaining ingredients except peaches, and mix well.

To peel peaches, drop into a kettle of boiling water for one minute. Drain in a colander. Slip off skins. Halve, remove pits, chop coarsely. Stir into pot with other ingredients.

Simmer over low heat until thickened, about one hour, stirring frequently and gently. Fill hot sterilized jars. Water process 15 minutes; Remove jars from hot water and cool on rack. Check seals, label promptly.

Makes 6 eight-ounce jars

Fresh Hot Salsa

Ingredients
20 lb. ripe tomatoes
24 assorted hot peppers
6 medium-sized onions
12 tomatillos
4 cloves garlic, peeled
4 tablespoons salt
1 cup vinegar
¾ cup olive oil
½ cup each fresh cut basil, cilantro and parsley leaves

Instructions
Bring a large pot of water to a boil. Drop in tomatoes to scald briefly, then drain and remove skins. Chop finely and transfer to a large colander. Wearing rubber gloves, trim tops off peppers and chop coarsely. Add to the tomatoes. Chop the onions, garlic, and tomatillos finely; add to tomatoes and peppers. Stir in salt and allow to sit and drain for two to three hours.

After draining, give a few good stirs, then add the oil, vinegar and herbs. Transfer to a large pot and cook over medium heat until it bubbles. Enjoy fresh or pack into hot, sterilized jars and process for canning.

Makes 8 pints

Pumpkin Pie

Ingredients

1 ½ cups of cooked and mashed pumpkin
½ cup brown sugar
½ cup white sugar
1 tablespoon molasses
1/16 teaspoon powdered cloves
1 ½ teaspoon cinnamon
¼ teaspoon ground ginger
2 eggs, beaten
1 cup milk, scalded

Instructions

Mix all ingredients; pour into a pie shell. Preheat oven to 450° F and bake for 10 minutes. Reduce heat to 325° F and continue baking until knife comes out clean (about 40 minutes).

WINTER

Potato Leek Soup

Ingredients

¼ cup butter
4 leeks, roots and tops removed
3 medium potatoes, scrubbed and cut into ½ inch slices
1 celeriac knob, peeled and cut into one inch chunks
4 cups chicken or vegetable stock
fresh thyme, basil and / or sweet marjoram, to taste

Instruction

Melt butter in a stock pot. Slice leeks into one-quarter inch slices and add to stock pot. Sauté for five minutes or until golden. Add potatoes and celeriac and sauté for 5 minutes. Cover and cook three minutes. Stir in one cup stock, cover and continue cooking until potatoes are tender, about 25 minutes. Remove from the heat.

Pour vegetables and stock into a food processor or blender and puree. Return puree to stock pot and add remaining stock and herbs. Cover and simmer for 15 to 20 minutes. Serve hot.

Carrot Cake

Ingredients

1 pound carrots (approximately 3 cups, grated)
1 cup sugar
1 cup maple syrup
½ cup oil
4 eggs
2 cups flour
2 teaspoons baking powder
2 teaspoons baking soda
1 teaspoon salt
½ cup chopped pecans or walnuts

Instruction

Preheat oven to 325° F

Trim, scrape and grate carrots, then measure them and set aside. Combine sugar and oil in a bowl. Start beating. Add the eggs one at a time, beating well. Sift together the flour, baking soda and salt. Add this to the oil mixture while beating. Add grated carrots and nuts. Blend well.

Lightly oil three nine-inch cake pans. Shake flour lightly in pans. Pour batter into pans. Place in oven and bake 45 minutes.

Frosting

3 cups confectioners sugar
1 tablespoon pure maple syrup

Is there anyone, young or old, who doesn't love carrot cake? This three-layer version is sweetened with pure maple syrup.

1–8 oz. package cream cheese
4 tablespoons butter, softened
2 teaspoons vanilla extract

Sift the sugar into a mixing bowl. Mix in cream cheese, maple syrup, butter, and vanilla. Beat until smooth.

Grated Kohlrabi

Ingredients
2 to 4 kohlrabi knobs
1 small onion
4 tablespoons butter
¾ cup heavy cream
¼ teaspoon summer savory or sweet marjoram

Instructions
Trim, peel and grate the kohlrabi. Sprinkle with salt, then set in a colander to drain. After 30 minutes, squeeze the water out. In a skillet, over medium heat, melt the butter. Add the grated kohlrabi and the onion. Turn heat to low, cover and simmer for 10 minutes. Uncover, turn the heat to medium, add cream and herbs. Cook another two minutes.

Brussels Sprouts with Chestnuts

Ingredients
1 pound Brussels sprouts
4 tablespoons butter
2 cups braised chestnuts
Salt and pepper to taste

Instructions
Trim and wash Brussels sprouts, and steam or blanch until tender. Melt butter in a large saucepan, add Brussels sprouts and chestnuts, and heat through. Season with salt and pepper.

To braise chestnuts
2 cups peeled chestnuts
1 cup chicken broth
2 tablespoons butter

Bring all ingredients to a boil. Reduce heat, cover and simmer for 20 to 30 minutes until chestnuts are tender but not mushy. Now they combine with the Brussels sprouts.

Serves 6 (side dish)

This colorful and unusual salad features a lively combination of beets, apples, goat cheese and walnuts: perfect winter fare!

Beet & Walnut Salad

Ingredients
6 to 8 assorted beets, cooked and peeled
2 tart apples, cored
½ cup feta or goat cheese
½ cup walnuts
⅓ cup thinly sliced scallions
⅓ cup basic vinaigrette dressing
¼ cup flat-leafed parsley

Instructions
Slice beets and cut apples into wedges and mix together in a bowl with cheese, walnuts, scallions and parsley. Drizzle with vinaigrette and stir to coat. Serve on a bed of butterhead lettuce.

Celeriac Remoulade

Ingredients
½ cup mayonnaise (preferably homemade)
1 tablespoon Dijon mustard
2 tablespoons finely minced parsley
2 tablespoons finely minced tarragon

Opposite This hearty, main course pie features the pungent flavor of leeks and horseradish, just the thing for warding off winter's chill.

1 clove garlic, finely minced
2 sweet pickles, finely minced
2 young celeriac knobs, peeled and coarsely grated
    (2 to 2 ½ cups)

Instructions

In a medium-sized bowl, mix together mayonnaise, mustard, parsley, tarragon, garlic and sweet pickles. Add celeriac and toss until completely coated. Cover and chill until ready to serve.

Serves 4

Leek and Sausage Pie

Ingredients
6 leeks
2 cups chicken stock
4 tablespoons butter
4 tablespoons flour
salt and pepper
½ cup heavy cream
horseradish to taste
1 nine-inch pie shell, baked
4 pork sausages, cooked and sliced ¼-inch thick

Instructions
Trim the leeks by removing roots and green tops. Split lengthwise and wash carefully under the faucet. Cut into thin strips. In a stock pot, heat the chicken stock and cook leeks until just tender but not mushy, about 10 to 15 minutes. Drain, yet reserve stock for later.

In the stock pot, over low heat, melt the butter and blend in flour, stirring to thicken. Slowly add the stock while stirring. Bring to a boil and cook for about 15 minutes, stirring frequently.

Meanwhile, preheat oven to 375° F. In the saucepan with sauce, add leeks, sausage and the heavy cream. Season with horseradish, salt and pepper. Pour into the pastry shell and bake for 50 to 60 minutes.

References

GLOSSARY

Acid soil   Any soil with a pH reading below 7.0 on a scale of 1-14; the lower the reading, the more acid the soil. See pH.

Alkaline soil   Any soil with a pH reading above 7.0 on a scale of 1-14; the higher the reading, the more alkaline the soil. See pH.

Alternaria   A common family of fungus diseases that cause blights and rots in garden plants, for example Early Blight in potatoes and tomatoes. Most pronounced in moist conditions when the spores are able to germinate readily on plant foliage and establish themselves there.

Annual   A plant that under normal conditions completes its entire life cycle in one season. See Biennial, Perennial.

Anther   The pollen bearing part of a flower's male sexual organ. With the filament, atop which it sits, it comprises the stamen.

Aphid   A small sucking insect, usually pale green, gray or black, but also yellow pink or lavender. They are less than a quarter inch long, pear shaped, and appear in great numbers at the tender growing points of the attacked plant. They are most easily recognized by the fact that they secrete at sticky fluid called honeydew, and by the ants that will often be found at the same site, appearing to "tend" the aphids. They can be controlled by knocking them from the plants with a hard stream of cold water or by spraying with insecticidal soap.

Apical   Pertaining the apex, or tip. An apical meristem is the growing point of a given plant. See Axillary, Meristem.

Apical Dominance   The tendency of the apical meristem to inhibit the growth of axial buds by the production of auxins, whose strength decreases in proportion to distance. Removal of the apical meristem therefore results in increased branching.

Asexual propagation   Reproduction without the recombination of genetic material via the mating of male and female sex cells. See Clone, Vegetative propagation.

Auxin   A plant growth hormone that in low concentrations promotes growth while in large concentrations it inhibits growth. Cell elongation rather than division is promoted, thus branching is inhibited by the presence of auxins. See also Apical dominance, Cytokinin, Rooting compound.

Axil   The upper, or inside angle of the junction of a leaf and stem, or where a smaller stem arises from a larger one.

Axillary   Pertaining to the axil, as in axillary bud, a potential growing point located in an axil. See Meristem.

Bacillus thuringiensis (Bt)   A species of bacteria that attacks soft bodied caterpillars and paralyzes their digestive system, leading to death. Additional strains of this microbial insecticide have been discovered or developed that attack other pests, and related species of bacteria have been found which attack others, such as Japanese beetles and grasshoppers.

Basal   In plants that form rosettes, the basal leaves are those that arise directly from the crown of the plant, and which often differ from leaves arising from the stem. See Crown.

Bedding plant   Any plant used to create so called bedding displays, often geometric and surrounded by areas of lawn or paving. The most important characteristic for bedding plants is absolute uniformity in color, height, habit and bloom period. The term is also loosely used to apply to groups of plants that are being raised in a greenhouse before being set out in the garden.

Beneficial insects   Insects that help rather than hinder our gardening efforts. They may do this by pollinating flowers, by eating harmful insects or parasitizing them, or by breaking down plant material in the soil, thereby releasing its nutrients. Some insects could be considered both harmful and beneficial, e.g.: butterflies, which are beautiful in their adult form but destructive when in their larval, or caterpillar form.

Biennial   A plant that under normal conditions takes two years to complete its life cycle, growing to full size in its first season, then flowering in its second season before dying. See Annual, Perennial.

Biodiversity   Short for biological diversity. A state in which an ecosystem, whether natural or managed, contains a wide range of species and individuals of diverse genetic makeup in complex relations to one another. It is widely held that such diversity and complexity lends long term sustainability to the ecosystem and is thus desirable both in nature and in gardens.

Blanching   The exclusion of light from whole or part of a plant to decrease the production of chlorophyll and enhance tenderness. Roots and stem may be buried; leaves tied in a bundle to protect flower buds, or themselves covered with a pot or other container to blanch.

Bolting   The premature formation of flowering stalks, especially on plants grown for their leaves or roots, lowering harvest quality.

Borer   A pest which bores into the stems of plants, usually a larva such as a grub, caterpillar, or maggot. Symptoms often include an entrance hole and wilt on stem portions beyond. They can be controlled by digging out the pest, injecting an appropriate botanical or microbial insecticide, or by pruning the plant below the damage and destroying it with the pest intact.

Botrytis   Also known as gray mold. A fungal disease that is promoted by cool, moist weather. Symptoms appear as water soaked, blighted areas on flowers, stems or leaves with a moldy gray growth, hence the common name. Control by removing all infected plant parts and making sure the plants have sufficient room so that good air circulation is maintained around them.

Bract   A leaf that seems part of the flower cluster of a plant, or in the case of plants with insignificant flowers, may substitute for it in appearance by its bright coloring. Annual Clary (Salvia viridis) and poinsettia are two examples.

Bt Acronym for Bacillus thuringiensis, which see.

Bud A dormant, immature shoot from which leaves or flowers may develop. See Apical, Axillary.

Bulb An underground storage organ consisting of a thin, flattened stem section surrounded by layers of fleshy and dried leaf bases and with roots attached to its bottom. See also Corm, Tuber, Rhizome.

Bulbil Any small bulb like organ attached to a plant, usually on the stem at the apex or at an axil, or produced underground as an offset from a larger basal bulb.

Bulblet An underground bulbil, which see.

Callus The new tissue that grows over a plant wound or cut.

Calyx Collective name for all the sepals of a flower, the modified leaves which surround and protect flower buds.

Carpel See Pistil.

Cell The basic unit of living matter, consisting at a minimum of a nucleus within a mass of protoplasm that is enclosed within a membrane.

Chlorophyll A group of green pigments within the chloroplasts which effect the conversion of solar to chemical energy by the process of photosynthesis, which see.

Chloroplast The cell organelle in which photosynthesis takes place. See Organelle.

Climber A plant that climbs on its own, using twining, gripping pads, tendrils or some other method to attach itself to structures or other plants. Plants that need to be trained to a support are properly called trailing plants, not climbers.

Clone Botanical term for plants produced by vegetative, or asexual propagation, and which are therefore genetically identical to the parent plant.

Cold treatment Subjection of plants or seeds to low temperatures to enhance germination and/or flowering response. This technique is especially helpful in getting biennials to bloom in their first year. See Stratification, Vernalization.

Companion Planting The intermixing of different crops for the benefit of one or more of them. Thought by many to help with disease or pest control, but also a method of increasing beauty and productivity.

Compost Fully decayed vegetable matter with the appearance of soil that is used to improve both the texture and fertility of garden soil. Some composts are made with the addition of animal manures and mineral powders like lime, greensand and phosphate.

Corm An underground storage organ consisting of the swollen base of a stem, with roots attached to the underside. See also Bulb, Tuber, Rhizome.

Cormel A small, underdeveloped corm, usually attached to a larger corm. See Bulbil, Bulblet.

Corolla Collective name for all the petals of a flower, as opposed to the sepals, which see.

Cortex The usually corky tissue within stems and roots which serves as a storage area for food reserves and provides structural rigidity to the plant.

Cotyledon(s) The seed leaves, which are present before germination, as distinct from true leaves, which develop after germination. See also Monocot(yledon), Dicot(yledon).

Cover Crop A crop grown solely to occupy or improve the soil in a part of the garden that is not currently in crop production.

Crop Rotation The planting of crops from different cultural genetic groups on the same piece of ground in sequence for the purpose of balancing nutritional demands on the soil or breaking the reproductive cycle of pests and diseases.

Cross pollination The fertilization of the ovary on one plant with pollen from another plant, producing a progeny with a new genetic makeup distinct from either parent.

Crown The base of a plant, where stem and join, usually, but not always at ground level.

Cultivar Properly, a culti-vated var-iety of a plant that was developed through horticultural processes, rather than in nature. Its name is not part of the Latin name. See also Variety.

Cutting A section of stem or root removed from a plant and prompted to develop into a new plant, genetically identical to the parent plant.

Cutworm The larvae of several species of moths that pupate just beneath the surface of the soil. While in the larval stage they emerge at night and "cut down" seedlings, then devour them, leaving no evidence beyond the severed stem. Control is by putting one inch tall collars around the stem of newly set transplants so that the cutworms can't get to them. In addition,

some bran flakes moistened with Bt (make sure the label specifies that the kind you choose works for cutworms) can be left for them to eat instead, killing them.

Cytokinin A plant hormone that stimulates cell division rather than elongation. See also Auxin, Rooting compound.

Damping off Any of a number of fungal diseases which attack seedlings, causing the stem to wither at the soil line, collapsing the plant. There is no good cure for affected plants, but any remaining plants can be saved by removing all the diseased material and moving the seedlings to a warm, bright, airy location. Proper thinning and avoidance of over watering, especially during cloudy periods if the best preventive.

Daylength Flower initiation in many plants is affected the relation between day length and night length. Those that form flower buds only when the day length is less than a given amount are called short day plants; those that bud only if the day length exceeds a given amount are called long day plants. The critical length differs widely among species, however and cannot be specified overall. Day neutral plants flower after a certain period of vegetative growth regardless of day or night length.

Desiccant A material such as sand or silica gel that is used instead of hanging in a warm dark place to dry flowers for long term preservation.

Determinate The final size of the plant is genetically "determined". In practical terms this means a bush form plant; technically, it means that the main stem ends in a flower cluster rather than a vegetative shoot. See Indeterminate.

Dicot Any plant that has two cotyledons, or seed leaves. See Monocot.

Dioecious Having male and female sex organs on separate plants. See Monoecious.

Disbudding The removal of axillary buds from a plant to force all its energy into the apical bud, usually to increase the size of the resulting flower, usually for exhibition.

Division The breaking or cutting apart of the crown of a plant for the purpose of producing additional plants, all genetically identical to the parent plant.

Embryo The dormant, immature plant within each seed.

Endosperm The food storage tissue within a seed.

Epidermis The outermost layer of cells in herbaceous plants, equivalent to our skin.

Espalier Trained fruit trees supported, at least initially, by metal or wooden structures, to form a narrow hedge or fence. Espaliers are often trained to grow flat along the south face of a stone of masonry wall so the mass of the wall holds heat over night, thus causing the fruit to mature early.

Fertilizer Any material containing significant quantities of plant nutrients, especially Nitrogen (N), Phosphorus (P) and Postassium (K). Commercially prepared fertilizers are required to have their analysis of at least these three nutrients printed on the container.

Fibrous root A root system that branches in all directions, often directly from the crown of the plant, rather than branching in a hierarchical fashion from a central root. See also Tap root.

Filament Thread like stem on which the pollen bearing anther is held. See Anther.

Flower Specialize organ of the plant consisting of the reproductive organs, often brightly colored or strongly scented to attract insects for the purpose of fertilization.

Foliar feeding Fertilization of plant through application of a fine mist containing nutrients directly to the leaves.

Full Slip The point at which some melons separate easily from the vine, a sign of ripeness. Some types of melons, such as the French Charentais, do not slip at maturity, but remain attached to the vine.

Fungicide Any material capable of killing fungi. Sulfur and copper sulfate are two common mineral fungicides.

Fusarium A common family of fungus diseases that cause wilts and blights in garden crops. Soil dwelling, usually enters the plant through injured roots. Thrives in warm soil. See Verticillium.

Genus A group of related species, each of which is distinct, and unlikely to cross with any other. In the standard classification, a group of genera forms a Family, and a group of families an Order. See Species.

Germination The initial sprouting stage of a seed.

Glabrous Hairless, but not necessarily smooth.

Glaucous Covered with a powdery, blue-gray-green finish.

Green Manure A crop grown solely to be turned under, as a method of improving the soil by raising its organic matter content.

Greensand A natural, mineral material mined from ancient beds of the mineral glauconite for its content of potassium, which is released very slowly through the natural microbial activity of soil organisms.

Hardening off The process of gradually exposing seedlings started indoors to outdoor conditions before transplanting.

Heat Units (HU) A way of predicting the maturity of crops (especially corn) that is based on the calculation of the number of hours each day when the temperature exceeds 50(F, multiplying it times the number of degrees above 50(F and keeping a cumulative tally. Early varieties of sweet corn, for example, mature after accumulating about 1300 HU. See also Maturity, Days to.

Heeling in The temporary burying of the roots of newly dug plants to prevent their drying until the new planting site is prepared.

Herbaceous Dies back to the ground in winter. Generally applied only to non-woody biennial and perennial plants.

Herbicide Any material that kills plants, generally weeds. Some soaps have herbicidal properties.

Hirsute Covered with dense, coarse hairs.

Humidity The amount of water vapor present in the air. Relative humidity is the percent present in the air relative to the amount that the air could contain, given the temperature.

Hybrid The offspring of consciously, dissimilar pure strains of the same or related species. An F-1 hybrid is the first generation of offspring from such a cross and will often show increased vigor, as well as productivity and uniformity if the parent plants were carefully chosen.

Indeterminate The final size of the plant isn't "determined" by anything but the length of the growing season and protection from disease and pests; it may keep growing indefinitely. In practical terms this usually means vining. See Determinate.

Inflorescence Collective name for a group of individual flowers. The grouping can take many forms: a spike, where the blooms are closely packed along a vertical stem; an umbel or a corymb, where the blooms form a flattened dome; the complex hierarchical arrangement called a panicle, or the tightly packed disc flowers in the center of a daisy, called a capitulum.

Insecticidal Soap Specially formulated soap that causes dessication of an insect or bug's exoskeleton, but is relatively harmless to plants.

Insecticide Any material that kills insects. There are numerous botanical and mineral powders that are toxic to insects, as well as biodegradable chemicals such as soaps.

Internode The part of a stem that is in between nodes, which see.

Interplanting The mixing of two or more crops within the same planting space, whether for aesthetic, pest and disease control or simply to raise the yield per square foot. See also Companion Planting.

Juvenile That stage of development wherein the plant concentrates it energy on vegetative growth rather than on reproduction.

Kelp Meal The dried powder of seaweed used as a soil amendment for its broad trace mineral content.

Latin name The international, scientific name of a plant, agreed upon by botanists to apply uniquely to a particular species, and denoting its relationship to other, similar plants. The Latin name consists of two parts: the first, called the generic name, as it states the genus to which the plant belongs; and the second, called the specific name as it describes the species to which the plant belongs. If there is a variety or cultivar name as well, it follows the specific name. In written form, the generic name is capitalized, while neither the specific nor the varietal name is not; all are italicized. A cultivar name, if used, should be non-italic and enclosed within single quotation marks. Pronunciation of Latin names varies considerably from region to region around the world and should not be an inhibition to their use. See also Cultivar, Genus, Species, Variety.

Legumes A large family of plants including garden peas and beans which, through symbiosis with a soil dwelling bacteria, are able to extract free nitrogen directly from the atmosphere.

Lime A rock powder consisting primarily of calcium carbonate that is used to raise the pH (that is, to decrease the acidity) of acid soils. See pH, Acid, Alkaline.

Maturity, Days To For plants generally started indoors, the number of days from setting of transplants in the open garden until the development of the first harvest. For crops sown direct in the garden, the number of days from seedling emergence to the first harvest. See also Heat Units (HU).

Meristem Any growing point of both root and stem on a plant, where active cell division is taking place. There are both apical and axillary meristems. See Apical, Axillary.

Mesophyll The spongy inner tissue of a leaf, functionally similar to the cortex of stems and roots, where the raw materials-carbon dioxide and water vapor-are held during the process of photosynthesis within the adjacent palisade cells, which see.

Microclimate In general terms the character of a particular piece of land as influenced by purely local factors like elevation, direction and degree of slope, nearby buildings and vegetation such as trees and hedges, etc. Also: conditions right at ground level, out of the prevailing winds and under the effect of the covering plant canopy and the mass of the earth.

Monocot Any plant that has only one cotyledon, or seed leaf. See Dicot.

Monoecious Having separate male and female sex organs on the same plant. See Dioecious.

Nightlength See Daylength.

Nitrogen Major plant nutrient especially important for plants where foliage is the main interest.

Node That spot on the stem of a plant where both leaf and axial buds occur. The area of the stem between the buds is called the internode, which see.

NPK Acronym for the three major plant nutrients contained in manure, compost and fertilizers, and used to describe the amounts of each readily available. N is for nitrogen, P for phosphorus, and K for potassium (which was earlier called Kalium).

Nucleus The organelle within a cell that contains the cells chromosomes, and thus controls the various other cellular processes, including division into new cells.

Nutrient Any substance, especially in the soil, which is essential for, and promotes growth of plants. Generally applied to a group of a dozen or less common elements, especially nitrogen, phosphorus and potassium. See NPK.

Nutrient deficiency An inferior state of health in any plant brought about by insufficient amount of a given nutrient being present or available to the plant.

Open Pollinated In practical terms, non-hybrid; seed saved from garden plants not allowed to cross with nearby plants will produce plants quite similar to the parents for any number of succeeding generations.

Organelle A single purpose component within the cell.

Organic Matter That portion of the soil (usually less than 10%) that is comprised of living, or once living, organisms or their remains.

Organic Seed Seed harvested from plants grown without the use of synthetic fertilizers and pesticides, whether hybrid or open pollinated.

Ovary The part of a flower containing the ovules that will develop into seeds upon fertilization. With the style and stigma, it comprises the pistil, or female sexual organ. See Pistil.

Ovule Within the ovary, the body which will contain the seed upon fertilization. See Ovary.

Palisade cells A group of cells just beneath the epidermis of the leaf, which contain most of the chlorophyll in the leaf and are thus responsible for the bulk of the photosynthesis that occurs in the plant. See Photosynthesis.

Parterre A kind of formal garden design wherein geometrically arranged beds are planted with edgings and decorative arranged crops, whether ornamental or edible, or both. See also Potager.

Pathogen Any organism that causes disease, generally applied to bacteria, viruses, and less correctly, fungi.

Peat Partially decomposed mosses and sedges harvested from bogs and used as a component of soilless mixes, which see.

Peat pots Planting pots made from compressed peat. These are used for plants that resent disturbance, as at transplanting time the entire pot can be set out in the garden and the young plants roots will grow through the walls of the pot.

Pedicel A flower stem, as opposed to a leaf stem, or the peduncle, from which the individual pedicels arise. See Peduncle.

Peduncle The main stem supporting a cluster of flowers, as opposed to the pedicels, which are the stems of individual flowers. See Pedicel.

Perennial Any plant that lives more than three years. In general the term is applied only to herbaceous plants, which die back to the ground each year, as opposed to those with persistent, woody stem. See Annual, Biennial.

Perianth A collective term for the external parts of the flower: the calyx, or sepals, and the corolla, or petals.

Perlite A white, porous but sterile volcanic material that is used to improve the drainage of potting mixes. See also Vermiculite.

Petal A specialized leaf that surrounds the reproductive parts of a flower. Often colored to attract pollinating insects.

Petiole The leaf stalk which connects a leaf to the stem.

pH A symbol for the acid-alkaline balance of the soil. The balance is expressed as a number from 1 to 14, with 7 considered neutral. Thus a pH of 6 is acidic while a pH of 8 is alkaline. Higher numbers are more alkaline, lower numbers more acidic.

Phosphorus Major plant nutrient especially important for plants where flowering is the main interest.

Photosynthesis The process by which the chloroplasts in plant cells use sunlight to convert carbon dioxide from the air with water vapor to form carbohydrates that are used as the basic food stuff for the growth of the plant.

Picotee A pattern of flower petal coloration where the edges are a contrasting color to the body of the petal.

Pinching The removal of a growing tip from a stem, thus causing any axillary shoots or buds of the stem to develop.

Pistil The female sexual organ of a flowering plant, comprising the stigma, style and ovary. See Carpel.

Plug A type of seedling tray in which each seedling grows in an individual, tapered cell, thus reducing root competition with adjacent seedlings and minimizing transplant shock.

Pollen The male sex cells, which are held on the anther for transfer by insects, wind or some other mechanism to the tip of the stigma (which see) where they can then proceed to attempt fertilization of the female egg-cell, or ovule in the ovary at the base of the style.

Pollination The transfer of pollen to the stigma of a receptive flower. Fertilization does not occur until the pollen actually reaches the ovule at the base of the style.

Potager A French term applied to food gardens that are decorative as well as merely functional. See also Parterre.

Potassium Major plant nutrient especially important to the strength of roots and stems.

Pruning The removal of plant parts to improve the health, appearance, or productivity of the plant.

Rhizomatous   Having or capable of producing rhizomes.

Rhizome   A horizontal stem, usually underground, from which grow both leaves and roots. Usually persistent from year to year. See Runner, Stolon.

Rock phosphate   A naturally occurring mineral, calcium tri-phosphate which is mined and crushed for use as a fertilizer.

Root cutting   Section of root prepared for the purpose of vegetative propagation. See Cutting.

Rootbound   A situation where the roots of a plant have completely filled the container in which they grow, with further growth prevented until the plant is removed from the container.

Rooting compound   Commercial preparation of plant hormones used to promote rooting of stem and root cuttings. Usually available as a powder into which cuttings are dipped before planting.

Runner   A horizontal stem running along, but above the surface of the soil which produces roots and leaves wherever its nodes contact the soil. See Rhizome, Stolon.

Scarification   The nicking, sanding, or otherwise compromising the hard outer coating of seeds to increase their water intake and thus promote quick germination.

Seed   The fertilized, ripe ovule which contains the embryo from which a new plant may develop given the proper conditions.

Self fertile   Able to fertilize itself.

Self sterile   Unable to fertilize itself; requires cross pollination as the flowers are sterile to their own pollen.

Senescence   The aging process; a plant that is old and weak is said to be senescent. Also applied to describe a plant that is in the process of going dormant for the season, though technically only the parts that are dying, i.e.: the leaves are becoming senescent.

Sexual propagation   Production of new plants by seed, whereby the genetic material from two parent plants is combined, producing a new plant that is distinct, even if quite similar, to its parents.

Shattering   The process by which seed capsules, when ripe, spontaneous break open, scattering their seed.

Shearing   Wholesale cutting back of a plant, rather than selective pruning or deadheading. Often used to regenerate plants with many, small stems, where deadheading would be too time consuming. See Deadheading, Pinching, Disbudding.

Soilless mix   Any potting mix that is made without the addition of soil. Some common components include peat, bark, coconut fiber, vermiculite, perlite and sand.

Species   The basic unit of plant classification. Plants within a species have several characteristics in common, but most importantly, can cross with one another, but not normally with members of another species. The classification of species is quite fluid, with period revision by botanists a fact of life that gardeners are forced to contend with...

Stamen   The male, pollen producing part of a flower, consisting of the anther and its supporting filament.

Standard   A plant pruned so that it consists of a single, bare, vertical stem atop which is maintained a shaped mass of foliage, usually globular.

Stem cutting   Section of stem prepared for vegetative reproduction. See Cutting.

Sterile   Applied to plants: unable to reproduce sexually, that is to produce viable seeds. Applied to potting materials: free of disease organisms, or pathogens. See Pathogens.

Stigma   The part of the female sex organ which receives pollen from the anther. Supported by the style, through which it is connected to the ovary. Often sticky when receptive.

Stolon   A horizontal stem that runs along the surface of the soil, rooting where its tip contacts the soil. See Runner.

Stoloniferous   Having or capable of producing stolons.

Stratification   The exposure of seeds to moisture and low temperatures to overcome the dormancy of certain species, often from harsh winter climates. See Cold treatment.

Style   The part of the female sex organ that supports the stigma and connects it to the ovary.

Sub-species   A major division of a species, more general in classification than a variety.

Succession Planting   Replanting of the same crop at intervals throughout the growing season to assure a prolonged harvest.

Sulfur   A mineral element that has fungicidal properties. Sulfur dust is used to prevent many fungal diseases, and also functions as a minor nutrient for plants.

Tap root   A thick central root attached directly to the crown of the plant that branches little if at all. See Fibrous root.

Terminal bud   A plant's apical bud. See Apical.

Topdressing   The application of fertilizer, whatever its form, to the surface of the soil around established plantings.

Treated Seed   Technically, any seed that has been treated to enhance germination or reduce disease or pest incidence, but from the organic perspective, any seed that has been treated with a synthetic pesticide, usually in dust or slurry form.

Tuber   An underground storage organ, part of either the stem or the root of the plant. Stem tubers produce multiple buds on their surface from which shoots may arise the following season, while root tubers will sprout only from the point at which they were attached to the stem of the parent plant.

Turgid   Applied to cells and the plants which they comprise: fully charged with water. A damaging decrease in turgidity causes wilting.

Variety   A strain of plant having distinctive features which persist over successive generations in the absence of human intervention. Generally, variety applies to these naturally occurring strains, while Cultivar applies to horticulturally developed strains. See Cultivar, Latin name.

Vector   A transmitter or carrier of disease of infection.

Vegetative propagation   The use of plant parts such as cuttings (as opposed to seeds) to create new plants. New plants resulting from vegetative propagation are clones, genetically identical to the parent plants.

Vermiculite   A gray, mica-like material which when subjected to high temperatures forms a light absorbent material that is used to improve the drainage of potting mixes. See also Perlite.

Vernalization   Subjection of plants or seeds to a temperature regime that mimics the natural passage of the seasons. This is done to cause them to bloom out of season or at a younger age than would normally happen.

Verticillium   Soil dwelling fungus that attacks a wide range of garden plants leading to wilt of the plant and eventual death. Thrives in cold soil. See Fusarium.

ZONE AND FROST MAPS

Zone Map

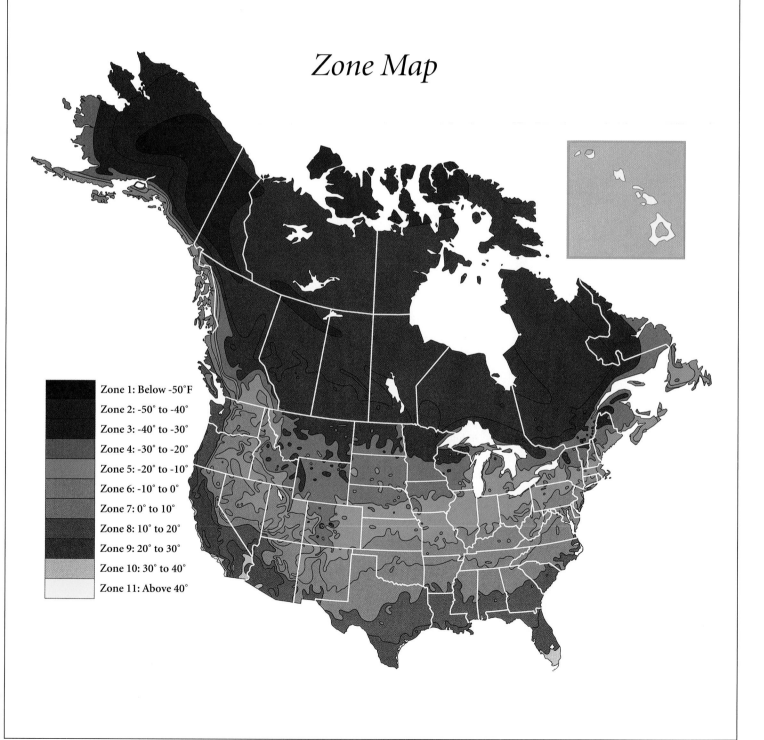

Zone 1: Below -50°F
Zone 2: -50° to -40°
Zone 3: -40° to -30°
Zone 4: -30° to -20°
Zone 5: -20° to -10°
Zone 6: -10° to 0°
Zone 7: 0° to 10°
Zone 8: 10° to 20°
Zone 9: 20° to 30°
Zone 10: 30° to 40°
Zone 11: Above 40°

Average Dates of Last Spring Frost

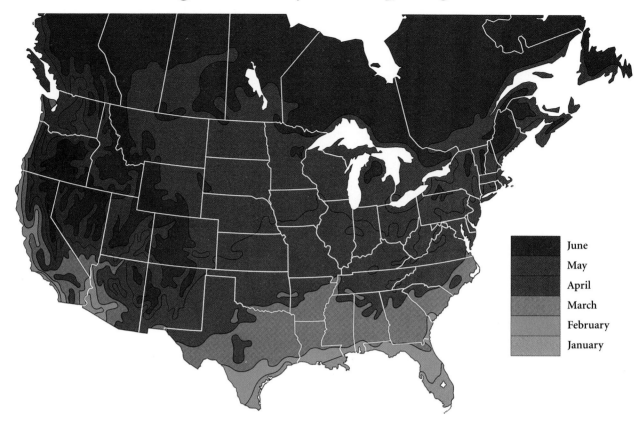

- June
- May
- April
- March
- February
- January

Average Dates of First Fall Frost

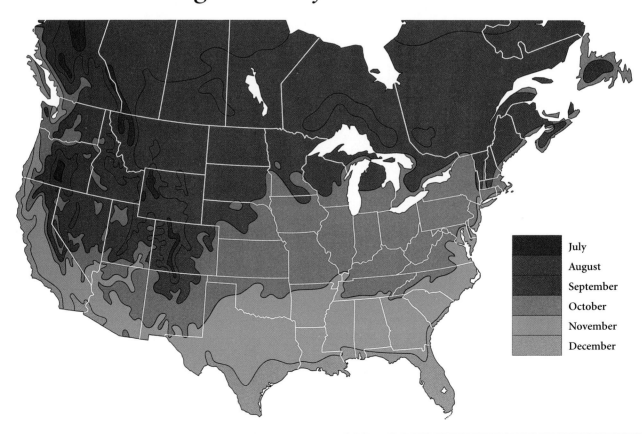

- July
- August
- September
- October
- November
- December

INDEX